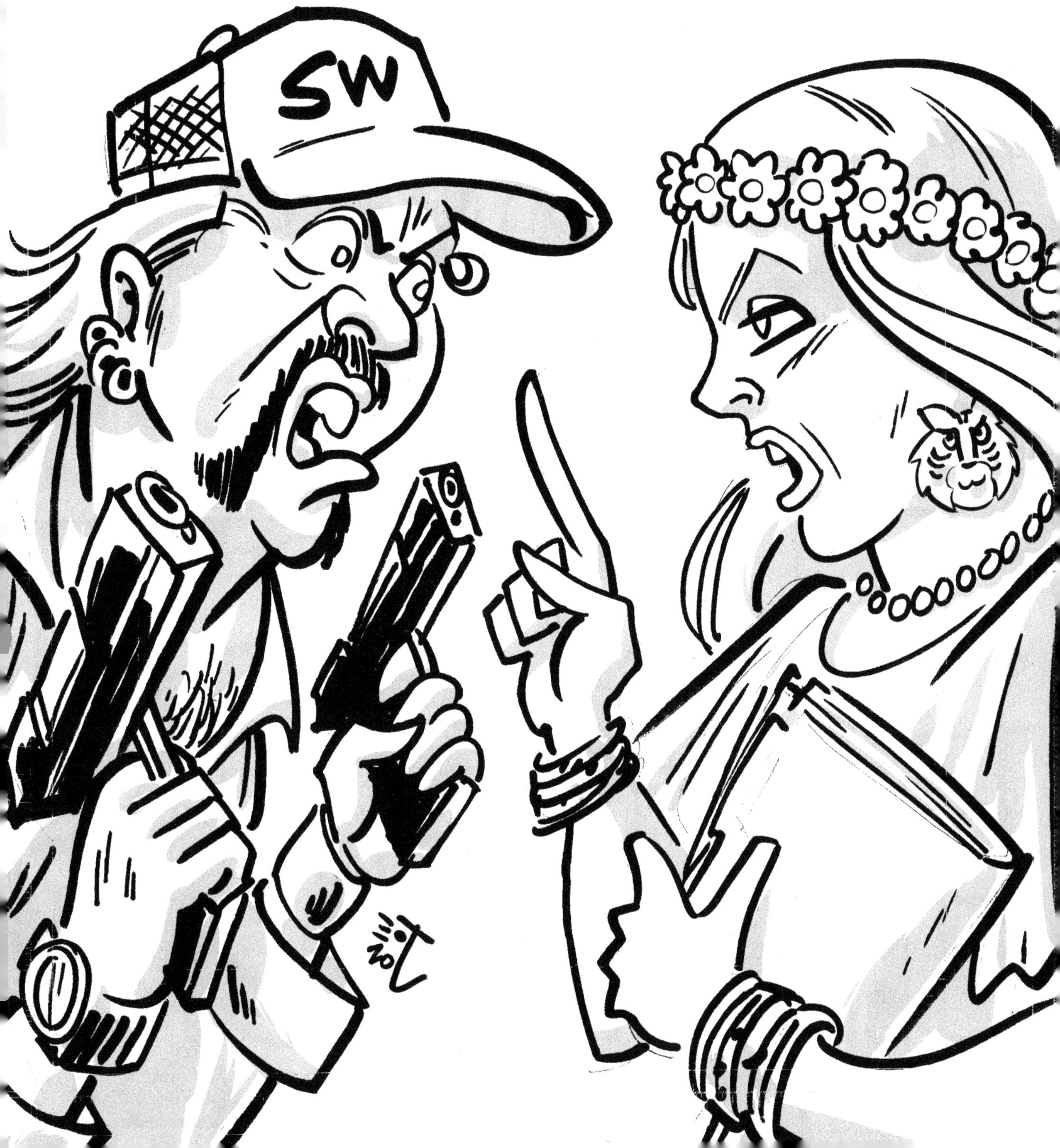
SW

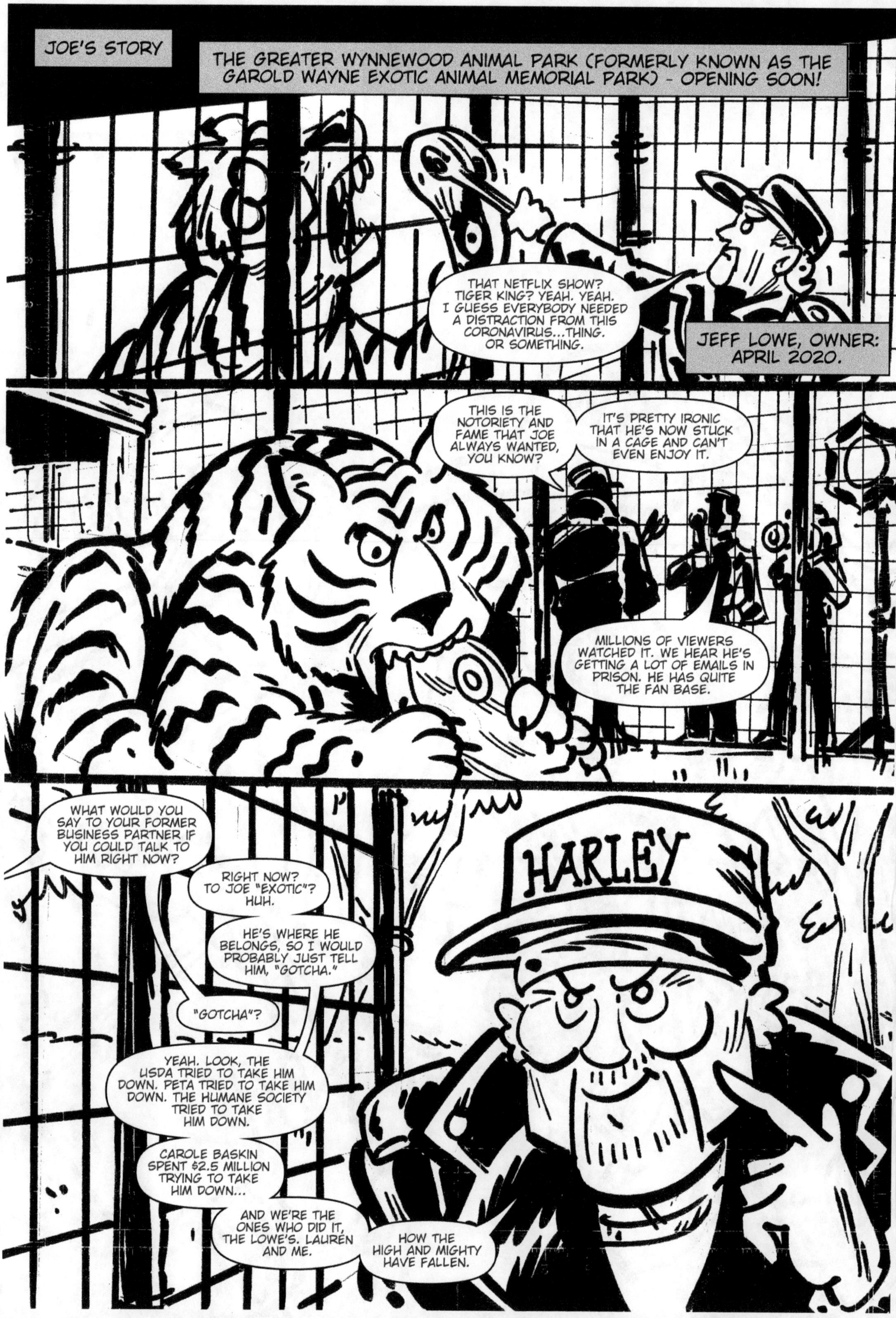
JOE'S STORY
THE GREATER WYNNEWOOD ANIMAL PARK (FORMERLY KNOWN AS THE GAROLD WAYNE EXOTIC ANIMAL MEMORIAL PARK) - OPENING SOON!
THAT NETFLIX SHOW? TIGER KING? YEAH. YEAH. I GUESS EVERYBODY NEEDED A DISTRACTION FROM THIS CORONAVIRUS...THING. OR SOMETHING.
JEFF LOWE, OWNER: APRIL 2020.
THIS IS THE NOTORIETY AND FAME THAT JOE ALWAYS WANTED, YOU KNOW?
IT'S PRETTY IRONIC THAT HE'S NOW STUCK IN A CAGE AND CAN'T EVEN ENJOY IT.
MILLIONS OF VIEWERS WATCHED IT. WE HEAR HE'S GETTING A LOT OF EMAILS IN PRISON. HE HAS QUITE THE FAN BASE.
WHAT WOULD YOU SAY TO YOUR FORMER BUSINESS PARTNER IF YOU COULD TALK TO HIM RIGHT NOW?
RIGHT NOW? TO JOE "EXOTIC"? HUH.
HE'S WHERE HE BELONGS, SO I WOULD PROBABLY JUST TELL HIM, "GOTCHA."
"GOTCHA"?
YEAH. LOOK, THE USDA TRIED TO TAKE HIM DOWN. PETA TRIED TO TAKE HIM DOWN. THE HUMANE SOCIETY TRIED TO TAKE HIM DOWN.
CAROLE BASKIN SPENT $2.5 MILLION TRYING TO TAKE HIM DOWN...
AND WE'RE THE ONES WHO DID IT, THE LOWE'S. LAUREN AND ME.
HOW THE HIGH AND MIGHTY HAVE FALLEN.
HARLEY

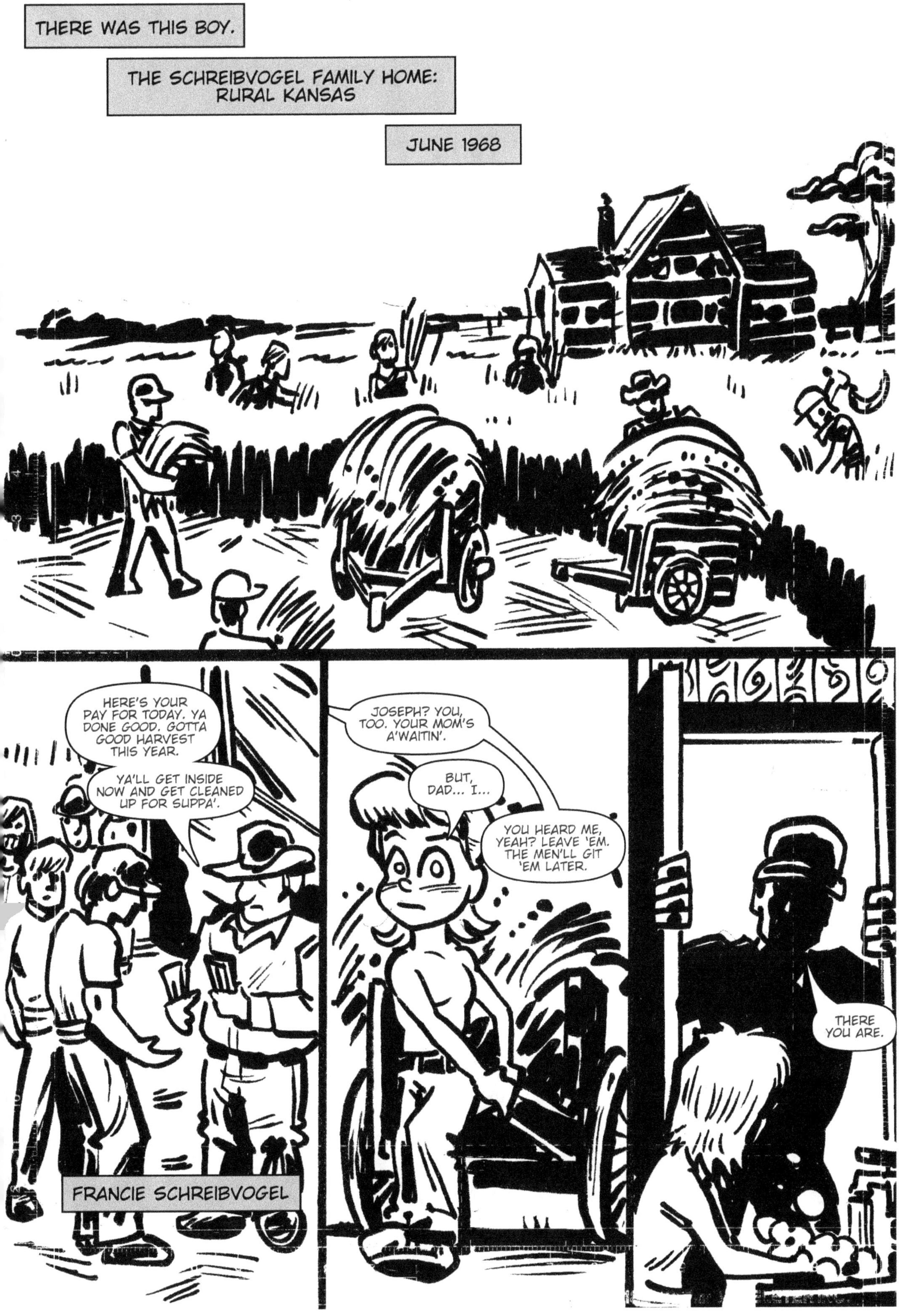
THERE WAS THIS BOY.
THE SCHREIBVOGEL FAMILY HOME: RURAL KANSAS
JUNE 1968
HERE'S YOUR PAY FOR TODAY. YA DONE GOOD. GOTTA GOOD HARVEST THIS YEAR.
YA'LL GET INSIDE NOW AND GET CLEANED UP FOR SUPPA'.
FRANCIE SCHREIBVOGEL
JOSEPH? YOU, TOO. YOUR MOM'S A'WAITIN'.
BUT, DAD... I...
YOU HEARD ME, YEAH? LEAVE 'EM. THE MEN'LL GIT 'EM LATER.
THERE YOU ARE.

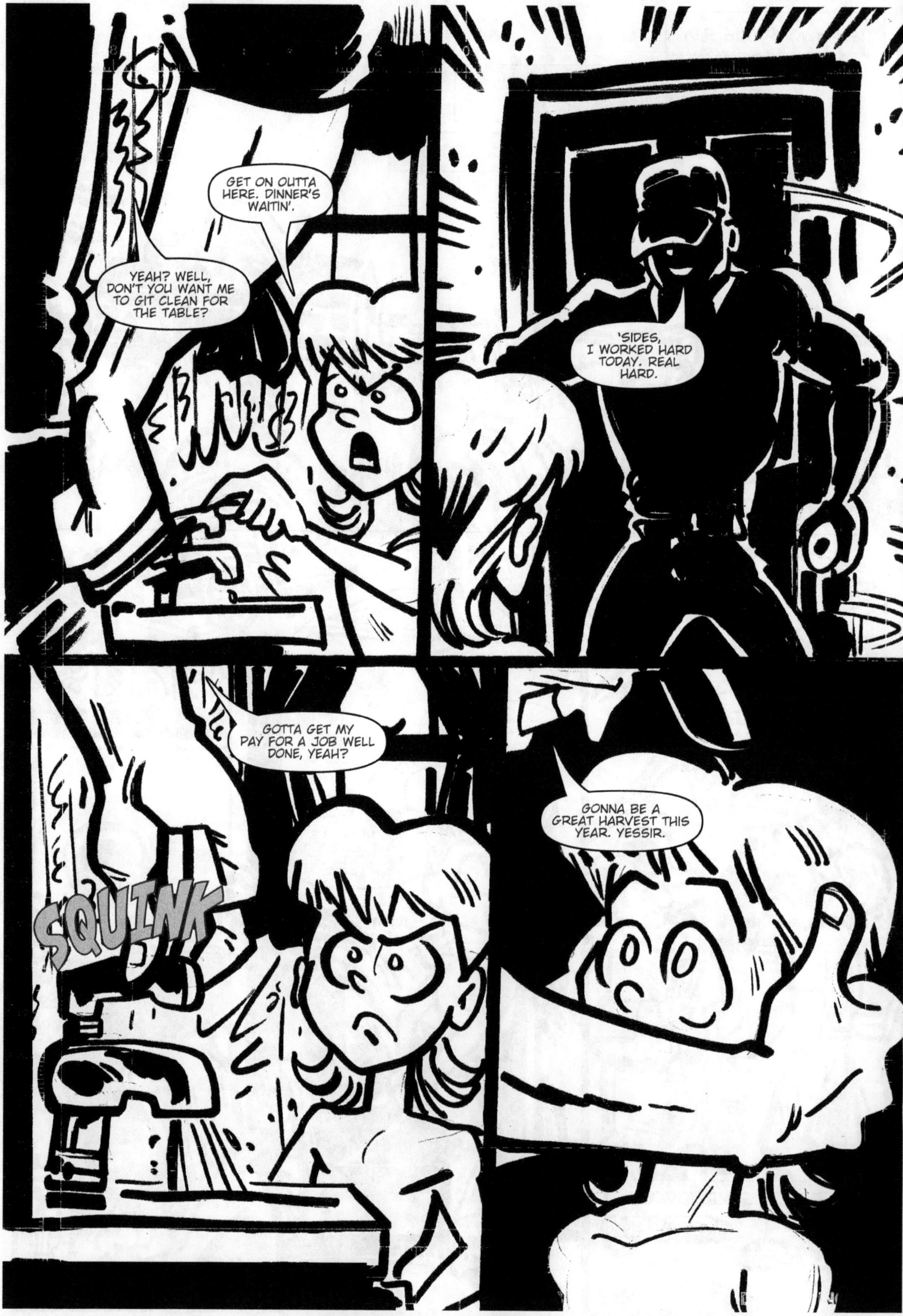
GET ON OUTTA HERE. DINNER'S WAITIN'.
YEAH? WELL, DON'T YOU WANT ME TO GIT CLEAN FOR THE TABLE?
'SIDES, I WORKED HARD TODAY. REAL HARD.
GOTTA GET MY PAY FOR A JOB WELL DONE, YEAH?
SQUINK
GONNA BE A GREAT HARVEST THIS YEAR. YESSIR.

THE BOY PREFERRED ANIMALS TO PEOPLE.
1973
<CHEEP CHEEP CHEEP CHU-REEP!>
<CHEEP CHEEP CHEEP CHU-
PAP
IT'S OKAY. DR. JOSEPH IS HERE. ALL BETTER. FLY AWAY NOW.

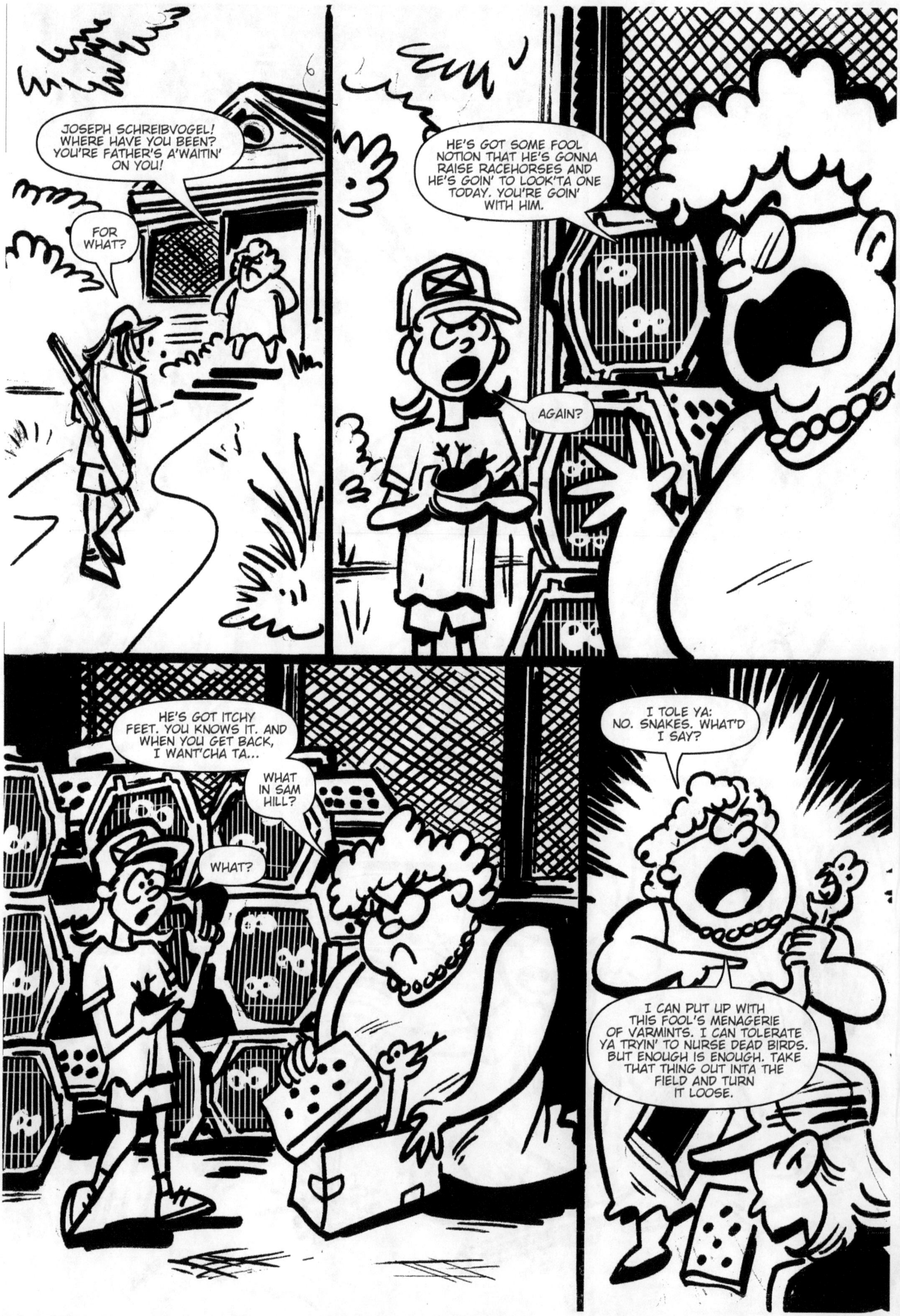
JOSEPH SCHREIBVOGEL! WHERE HAVE YOU BEEN? YOU'RE FATHER'S A'WAITIN' ON YOU!
FOR WHAT?
HE'S GOT SOME FOOL NOTION THAT HE'S GONNA RAISE RACEHORSES AND HE'S GOIN' TO LOOK'TA ONE TODAY. YOU'RE GOIN' WITH HIM.
AGAIN?
HE'S GOT ITCHY FEET. YOU KNOWS IT. AND WHEN YOU GET BACK, I WANT'CHA TA...
WHAT IN SAM HILL?
WHAT?
I TOLE YA: NO. SNAKES. WHAT'D I SAY?
I CAN PUT UP WITH THIS FOOL'S MENAGERIE OF VARMINTS. I CAN TOLERATE YA TRYIN' TO NURSE DEAD BIRDS. BUT ENOUGH IS ENOUGH. TAKE THAT THING OUT INTA THE FIELD AND TURN IT LOOSE.

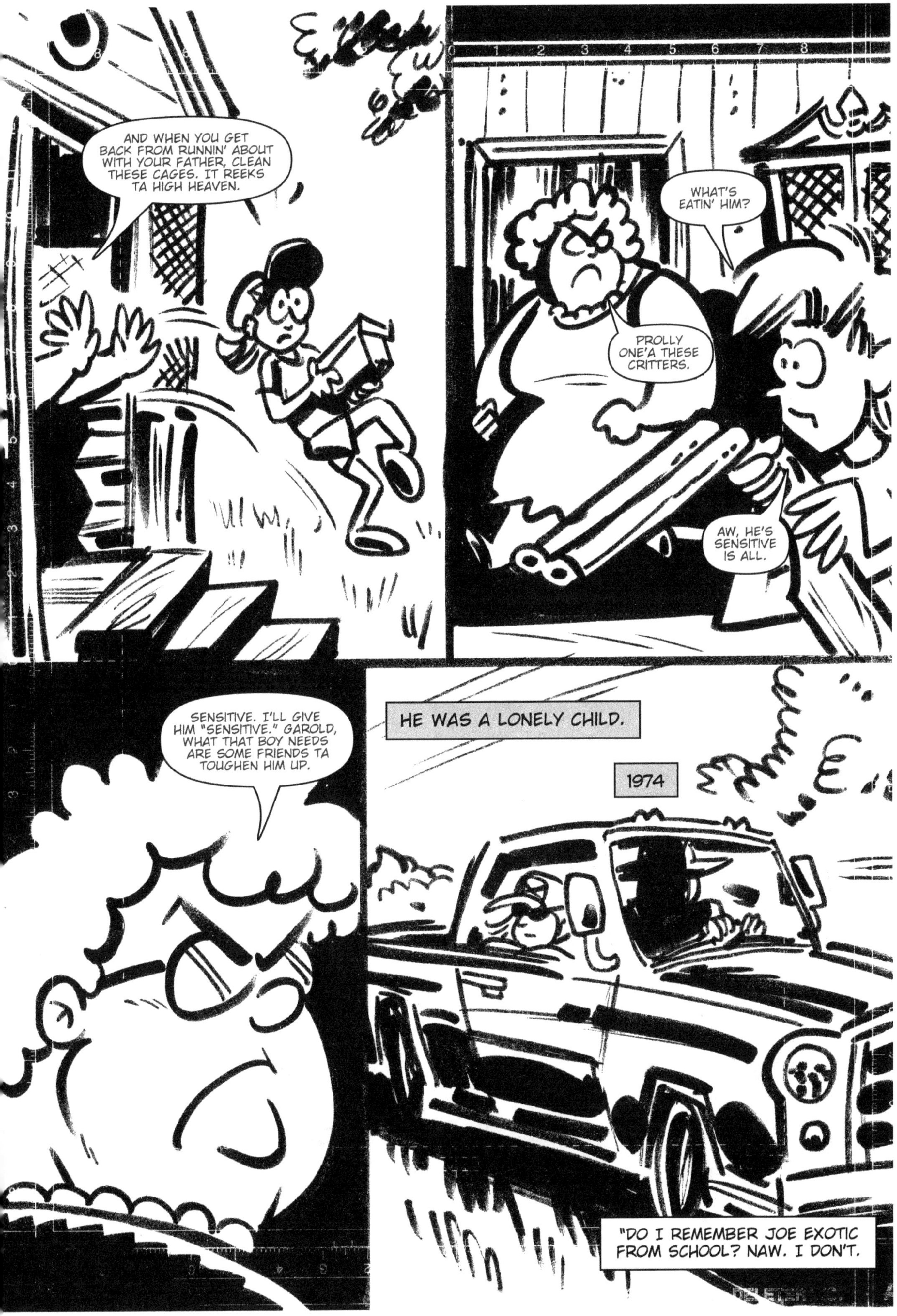
AND WHEN YOU GET BACK FROM RUNNIN' ABOUT WITH YOUR FATHER, CLEAN THESE CAGES. IT REEKS TA HIGH HEAVEN.
WHAT'S EATIN' HIM?
PROLLY ONE'A THESE CRITTERS.
AW, HE'S SENSITIVE IS ALL.
SENSITIVE. I'LL GIVE HIM "SENSITIVE." GAROLD, WHAT THAT BOY NEEDS ARE SOME FRIENDS TA TOUGHEN HIM UP.
HE WAS A LONELY CHILD.
1974
"DO I REMEMBER JOE EXOTIC FROM SCHOOL? NAW. I DON'T.

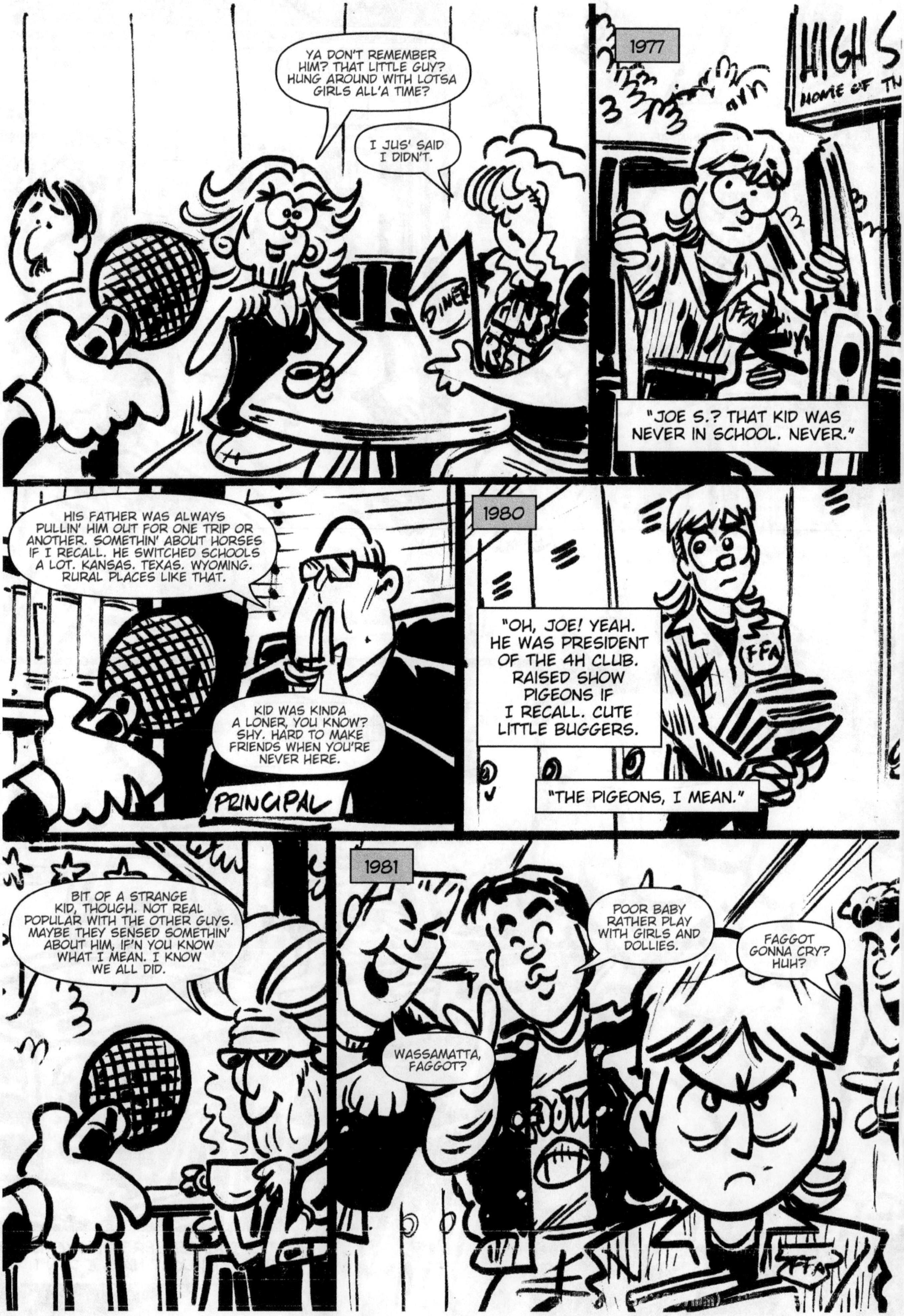
YA DON'T REMEMBER HIM? THAT LITTLE GUY? HUNG AROUND WITH LOTSA GIRLS ALL'A TIME?
I JUS' SAID I DIDN'T.
DINER
1977
HIGH S
HOME OF TH
FFA
"JOE S.? THAT KID WAS NEVER IN SCHOOL. NEVER."
HIS FATHER WAS ALWAYS PULLIN' HIM OUT FOR ONE TRIP OR ANOTHER. SOMETHIN' ABOUT HORSES IF I RECALL. HE SWITCHED SCHOOLS A LOT. KANSAS. TEXAS. WYOMING. RURAL PLACES LIKE THAT.
KID WAS KINDA A LONER, YOU KNOW? SHY. HARD TO MAKE FRIENDS WHEN YOU'RE NEVER HERE.
PRINCIPAL
1980
"OH, JOE! YEAH. HE WAS PRESIDENT OF THE 4H CLUB. RAISED SHOW PIGEONS IF I RECALL. CUTE LITTLE BUGGERS.
"THE PIGEONS, I MEAN."
FFA
BIT OF A STRANGE KID, THOUGH. NOT REAL POPULAR WITH THE OTHER GUYS. MAYBE THEY SENSED SOMETHIN' ABOUT HIM, IF'N YOU KNOW WHAT I MEAN. I KNOW WE ALL DID.
1981
POOR BABY RATHER PLAY WITH GIRLS AND DOLLIES.
FAGGOT GONNA CRY? HUH?
WASSAMATTA, FAGGOT?
FFA

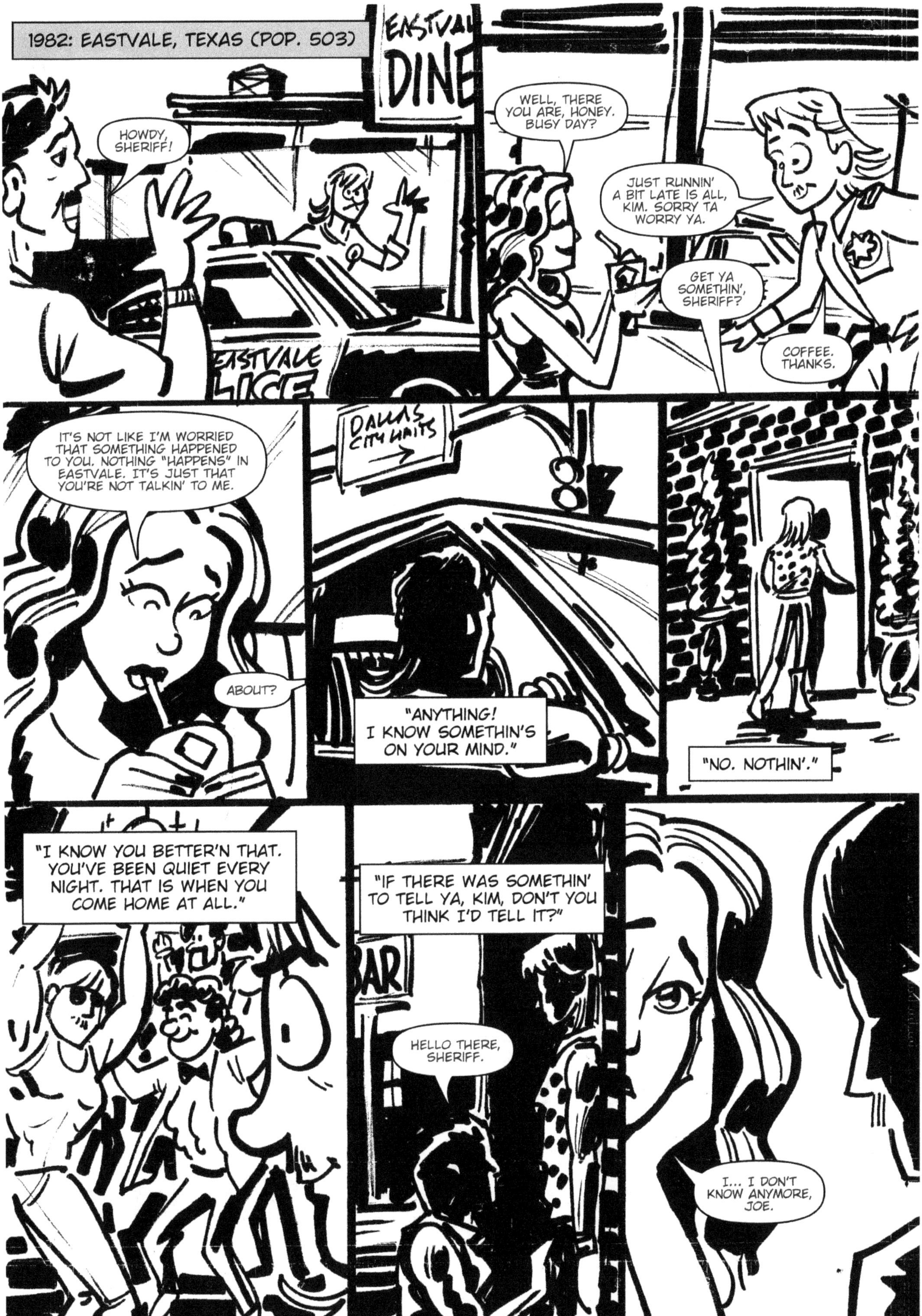
1982: EASTVALE, TEXAS (POP. 503)
EASTVALE DINE
HOWDY, SHERIFF!
EASTVALE POLICE
WELL, THERE YOU ARE, HONEY. BUSY DAY?
JUST RUNNIN' A BIT LATE IS ALL, KIM. SORRY TA WORRY YA.
GET YA SOMETHIN', SHERIFF?
COFFEE. THANKS.
IT'S NOT LIKE I'M WORRIED THAT SOMETHING HAPPENED TO YOU. NOTHING "HAPPENS" IN EASTVALE. IT'S JUST THAT YOU'RE NOT TALKIN' TO ME.
ABOUT?
DALLAS CITY LIMITS
"ANYTHING! I KNOW SOMETHIN'S ON YOUR MIND."
"NO. NOTHIN'."
"I KNOW YOU BETTER'N THAT. YOU'VE BEEN QUIET EVERY NIGHT. THAT IS WHEN YOU COME HOME AT ALL."
"IF THERE WAS SOMETHIN' TO TELL YA, KIM, DON'T YOU THINK I'D TELL IT?"
BAR
HELLO THERE, SHERIFF.
I... I DON'T KNOW ANYMORE, JOE.

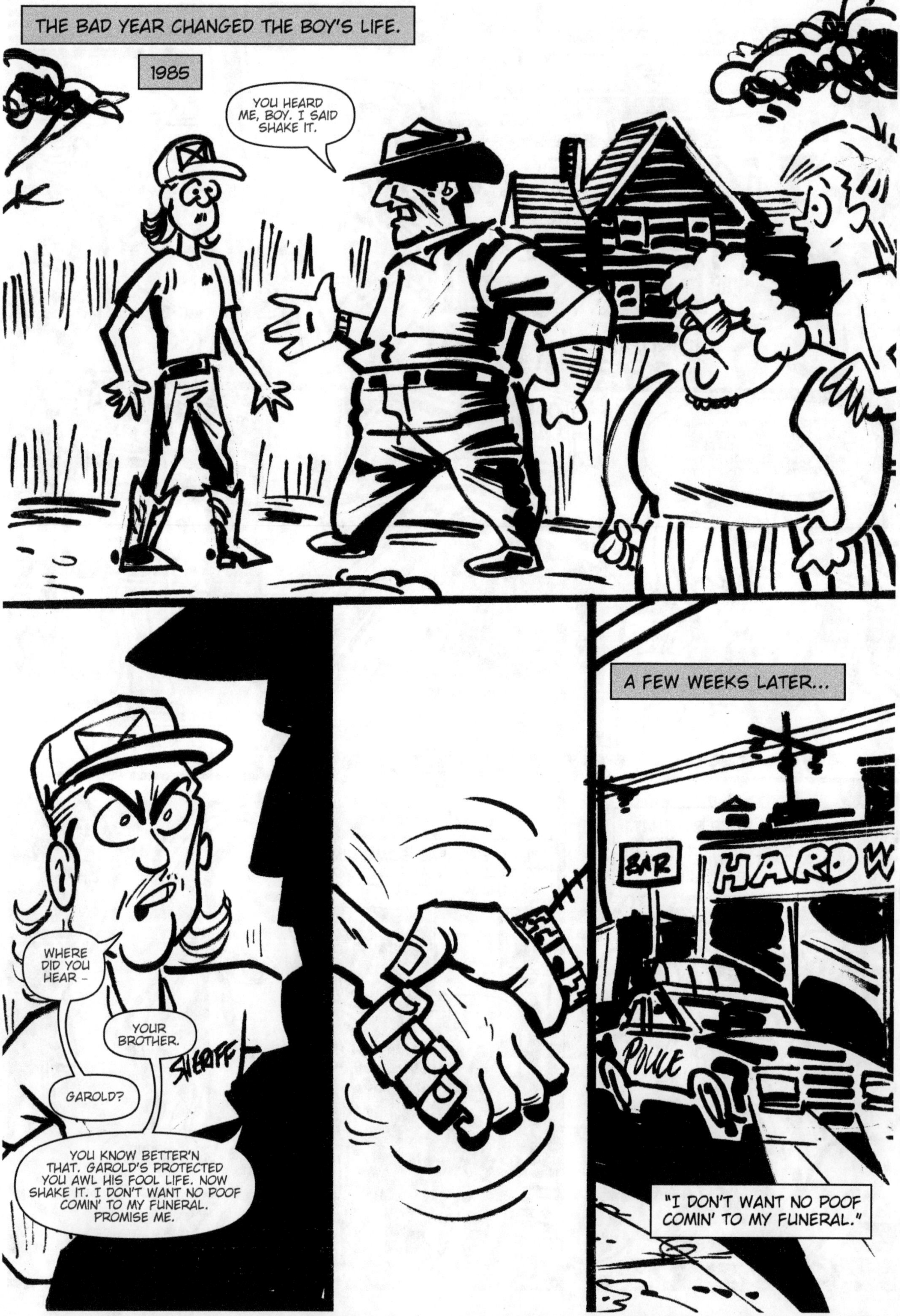
THE BAD YEAR CHANGED THE BOY'S LIFE.
1985
YOU HEARD ME, BOY. I SAID SHAKE IT.
WHERE DID YOU HEAR –
YOUR BROTHER.
SHERIFF
GAROLD?
YOU KNOW BETTER'N THAT. GAROLD'S PROTECTED YOU AWL HIS FOOL LIFE. NOW SHAKE IT. I DON'T WANT NO POOF COMIN' TO MY FUNERAL. PROMISE ME.
A FEW WEEKS LATER...
BAR
HARDW
POLICE
"I DON'T WANT NO POOF COMIN' TO MY FUNERAL."

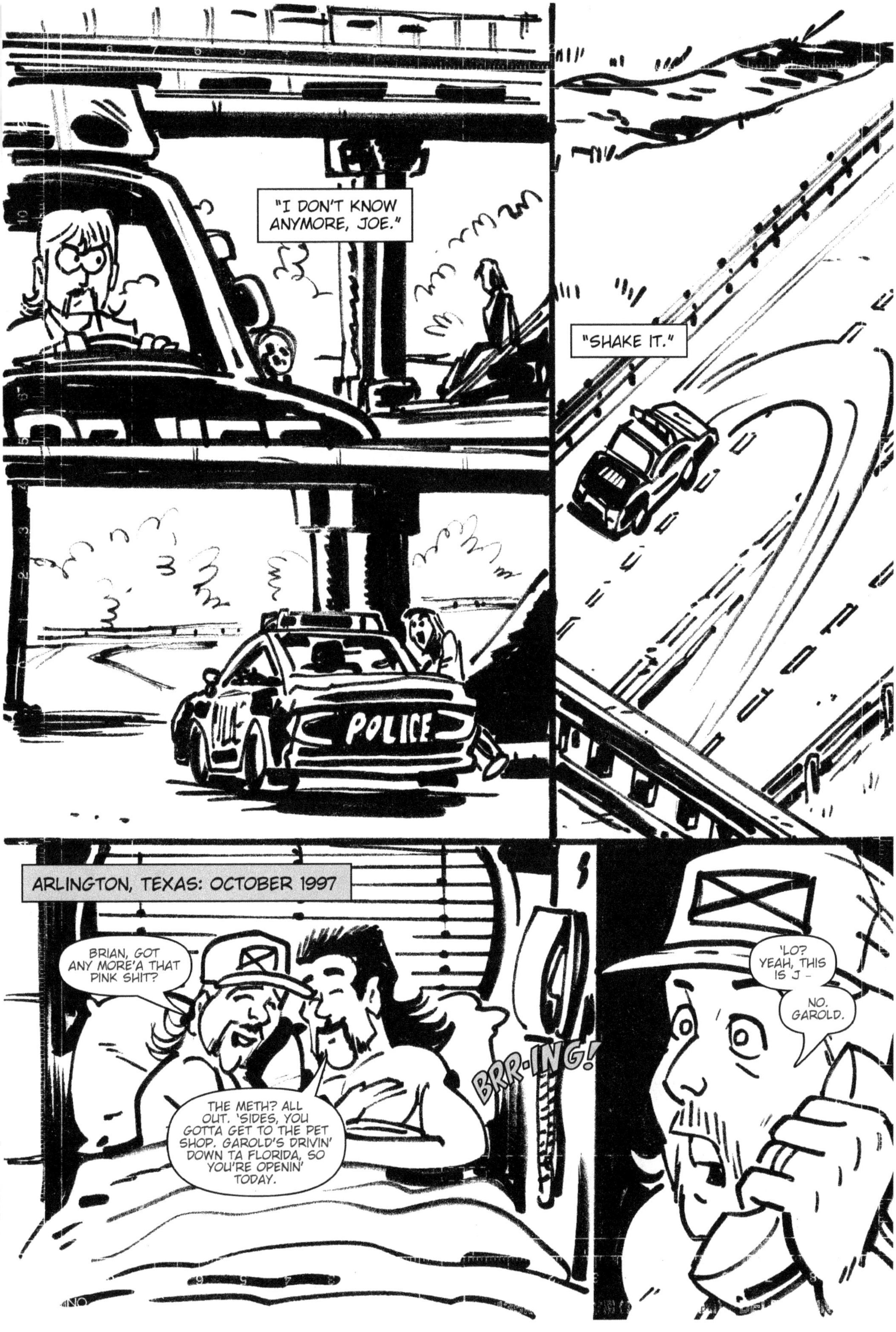
"I DON'T KNOW ANYMORE, JOE."
POLICE
"SHAKE IT."
ARLINGTON, TEXAS: OCTOBER 1997
BRIAN, GOT ANY MORE'A THAT PINK SHIT?
THE METH? ALL OUT. 'SIDES, YOU GOTTA GET TO THE PET SHOP. GAROLD'S DRIVIN' DOWN TA FLORIDA, SO YOU'RE OPENIN' TODAY.
BRR-ING!
'LO? YEAH, THIS IS J -
NO. GAROLD.

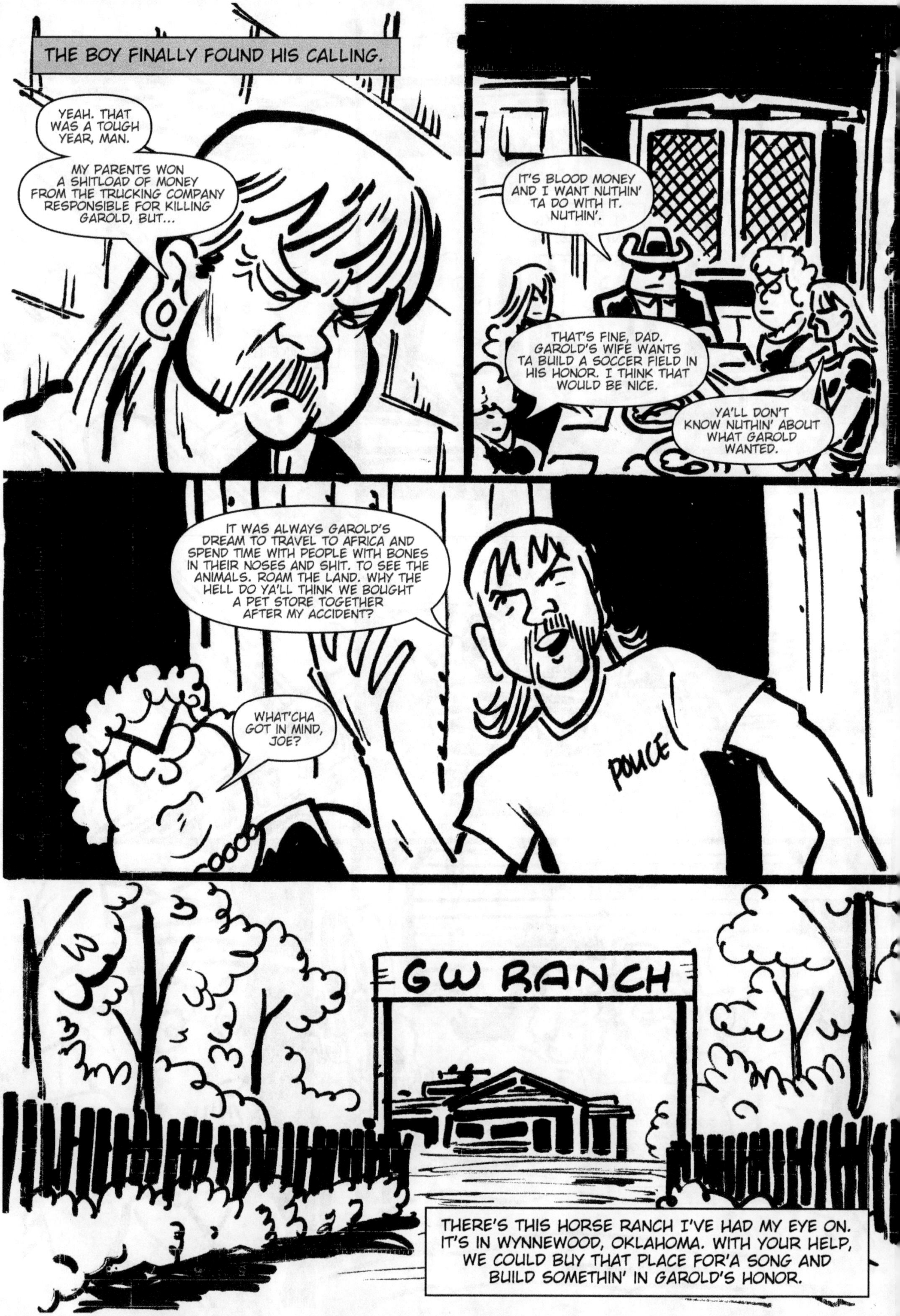
THE BOY FINALLY FOUND HIS CALLING.
YEAH. THAT WAS A TOUGH YEAR, MAN.
MY PARENTS WON A SHITLOAD OF MONEY FROM THE TRUCKING COMPANY RESPONSIBLE FOR KILLING GAROLD, BUT...
IT'S BLOOD MONEY AND I WANT NUTHIN' TA DO WITH IT. NUTHIN'.
THAT'S FINE, DAD. GAROLD'S WIFE WANTS TA BUILD A SOCCER FIELD IN HIS HONOR. I THINK THAT WOULD BE NICE.
YA'LL DON'T KNOW NUTHIN' ABOUT WHAT GAROLD WANTED.
IT WAS ALWAYS GAROLD'S DREAM TO TRAVEL TO AFRICA AND SPEND TIME WITH PEOPLE WITH BONES IN THEIR NOSES AND SHIT. TO SEE THE ANIMALS. ROAM THE LAND. WHY THE HELL DO YA'LL THINK WE BOUGHT A PET STORE TOGETHER AFTER MY ACCIDENT?
WHAT'CHA GOT IN MIND, JOE?
POLICE
GW RANCH
THERE'S THIS HORSE RANCH I'VE HAD MY EYE ON. IT'S IN WYNNEWOOD, OKLAHOMA. WITH YOUR HELP, WE COULD BUY THAT PLACE FOR'A SONG AND BUILD SOMETHIN' IN GAROLD'S HONOR.

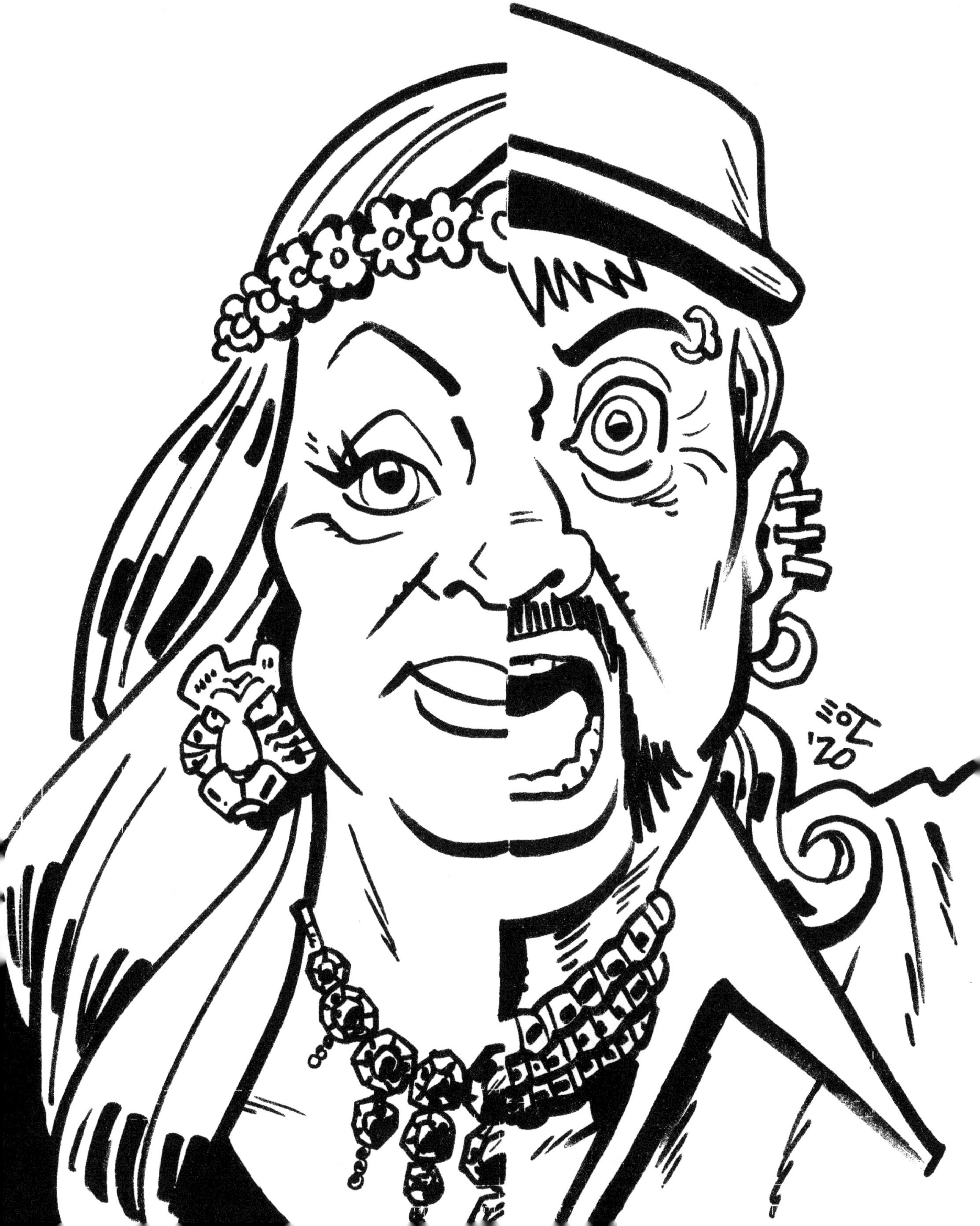
JOE '20

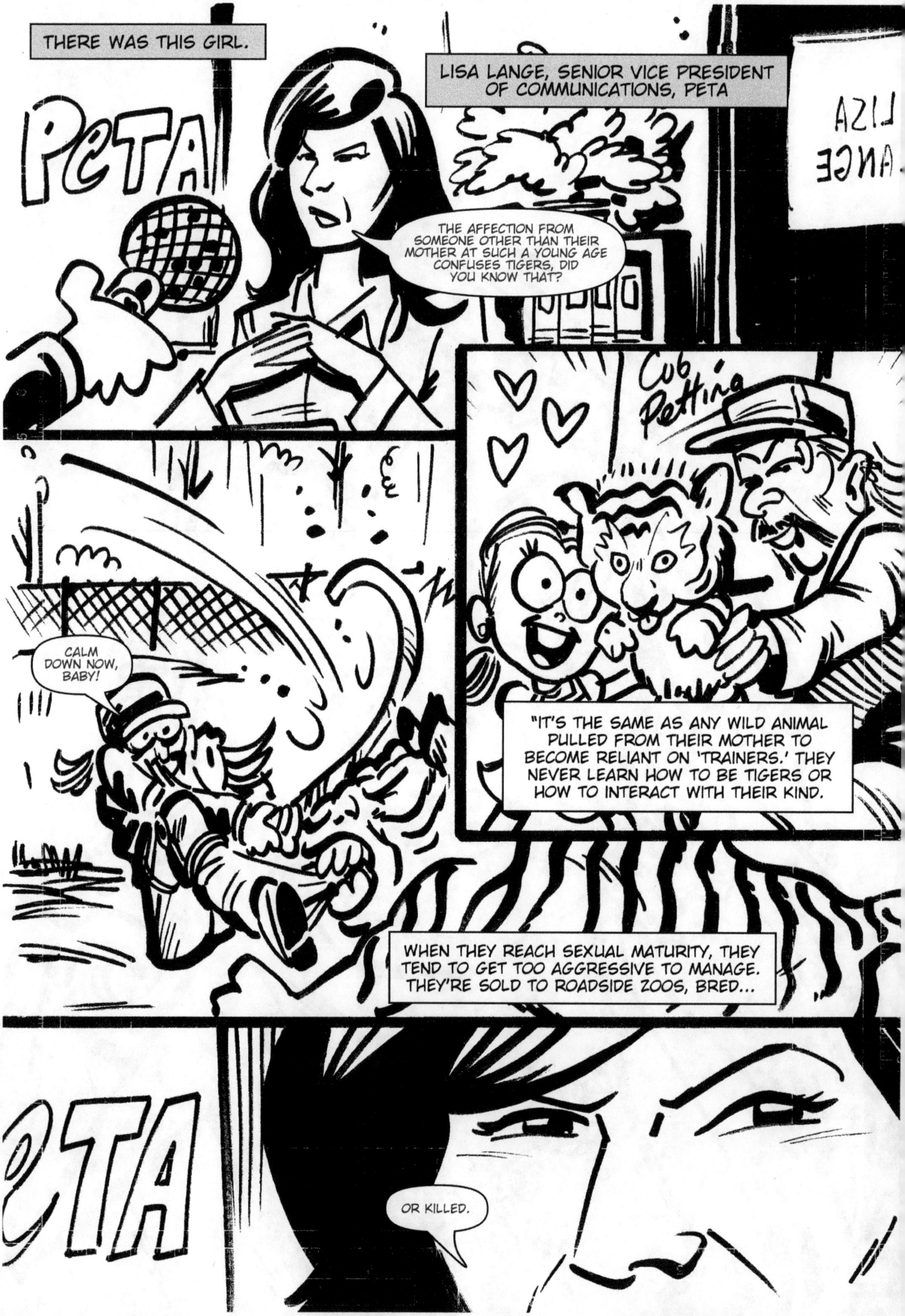
THERE WAS THIS GIRL.
PETA
LISA LANGE, SENIOR VICE PRESIDENT OF COMMUNICATIONS, PETA
THE AFFECTION FROM SOMEONE OTHER THAN THEIR MOTHER AT SUCH A YOUNG AGE CONFUSES TIGERS, DID YOU KNOW THAT?
Cub Petting
"IT'S THE SAME AS ANY WILD ANIMAL PULLED FROM THEIR MOTHER TO BECOME RELIANT ON 'TRAINERS.' THEY NEVER LEARN HOW TO BE TIGERS OR HOW TO INTERACT WITH THEIR KIND.
CALM DOWN NOW, BABY!
WHEN THEY REACH SEXUAL MATURITY, THEY TEND TO GET TOO AGGRESSIVE TO MANAGE. THEY'RE SOLD TO ROADSIDE ZOOS, BRED...
OR KILLED.

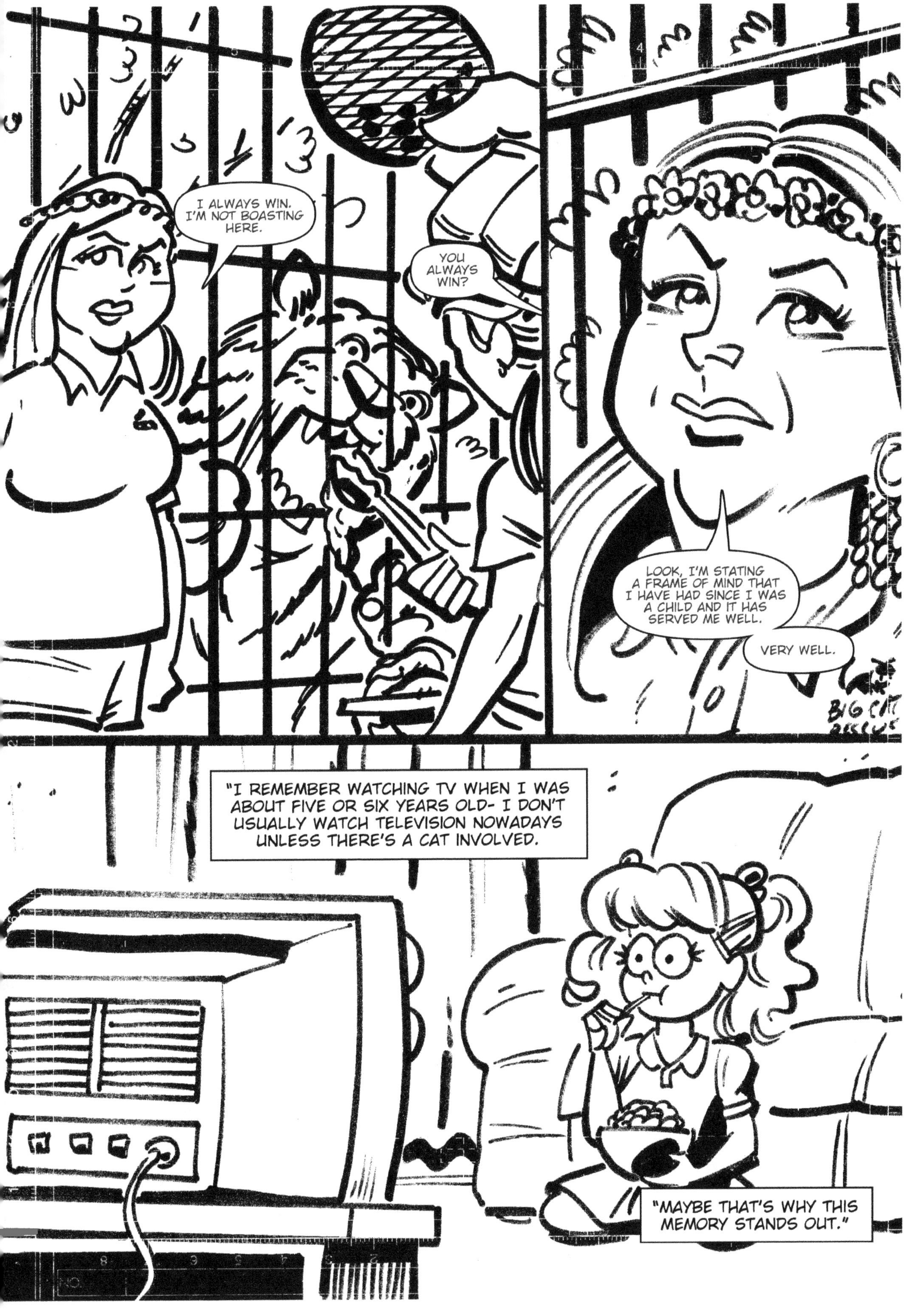
I ALWAYS WIN. I'M NOT BOASTING HERE.
YOU ALWAYS WIN?
LOOK, I'M STATING A FRAME OF MIND THAT I HAVE HAD SINCE I WAS A CHILD AND IT HAS SERVED ME WELL.
VERY WELL.
"I REMEMBER WATCHING TV WHEN I WAS ABOUT FIVE OR SIX YEARS OLD- I DON'T USUALLY WATCH TELEVISION NOWADAYS UNLESS THERE'S A CAT INVOLVED.
"MAYBE THAT'S WHY THIS MEMORY STANDS OUT."

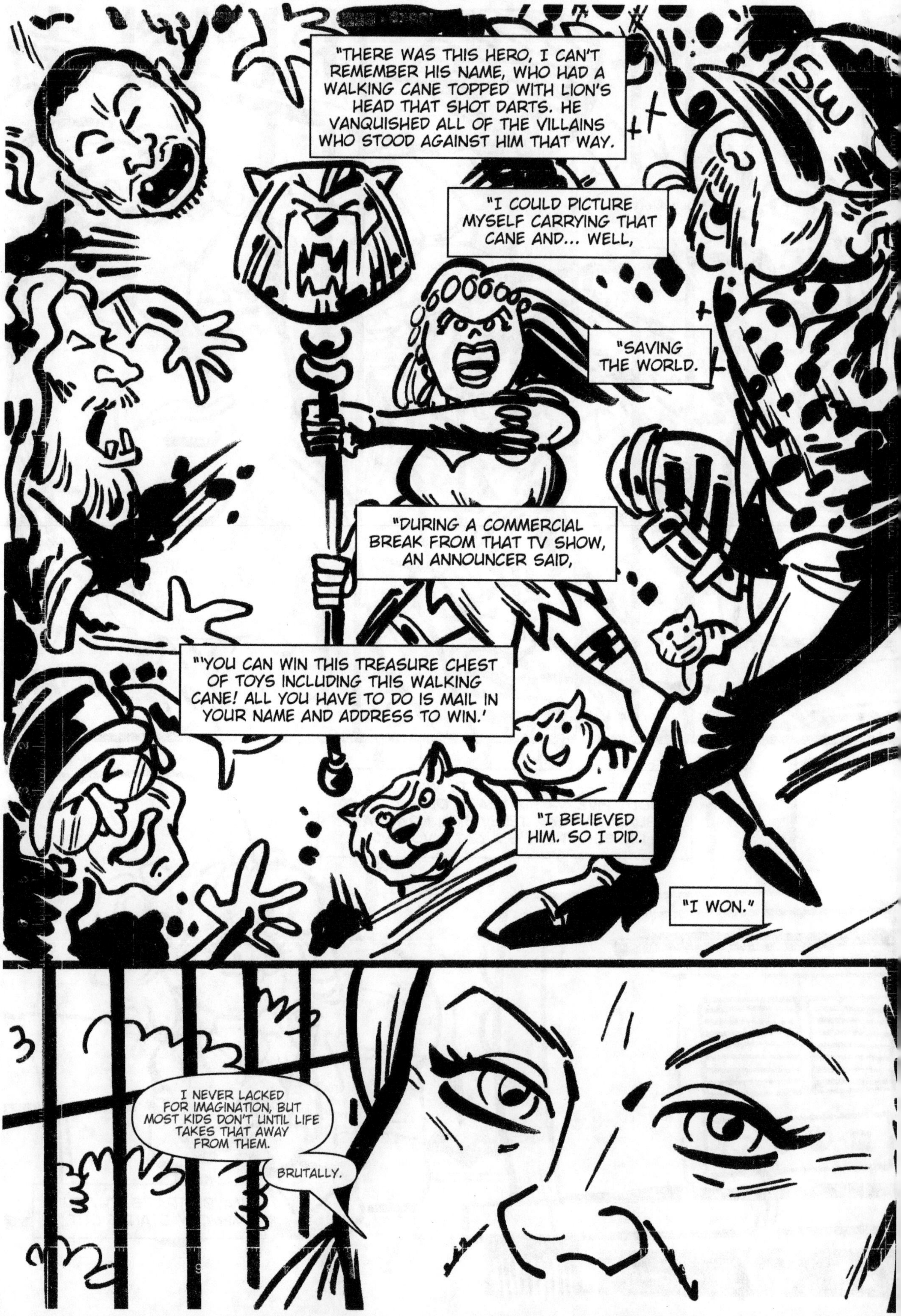
"THERE WAS THIS HERO, I CAN'T REMEMBER HIS NAME, WHO HAD A WALKING CANE TOPPED WITH LION'S HEAD THAT SHOT DARTS. HE VANQUISHED ALL OF THE VILLAINS WHO STOOD AGAINST HIM THAT WAY.
"I COULD PICTURE MYSELF CARRYING THAT CANE AND... WELL,
"SAVING THE WORLD.
"DURING A COMMERCIAL BREAK FROM THAT TV SHOW, AN ANNOUNCER SAID,
"'YOU CAN WIN THIS TREASURE CHEST OF TOYS INCLUDING THIS WALKING CANE! ALL YOU HAVE TO DO IS MAIL IN YOUR NAME AND ADDRESS TO WIN.'
"I BELIEVED HIM. SO I DID.
"I WON."
I NEVER LACKED FOR IMAGINATION, BUT MOST KIDS DON'T UNTIL LIFE TAKES THAT AWAY FROM THEM.
BRUTALLY.

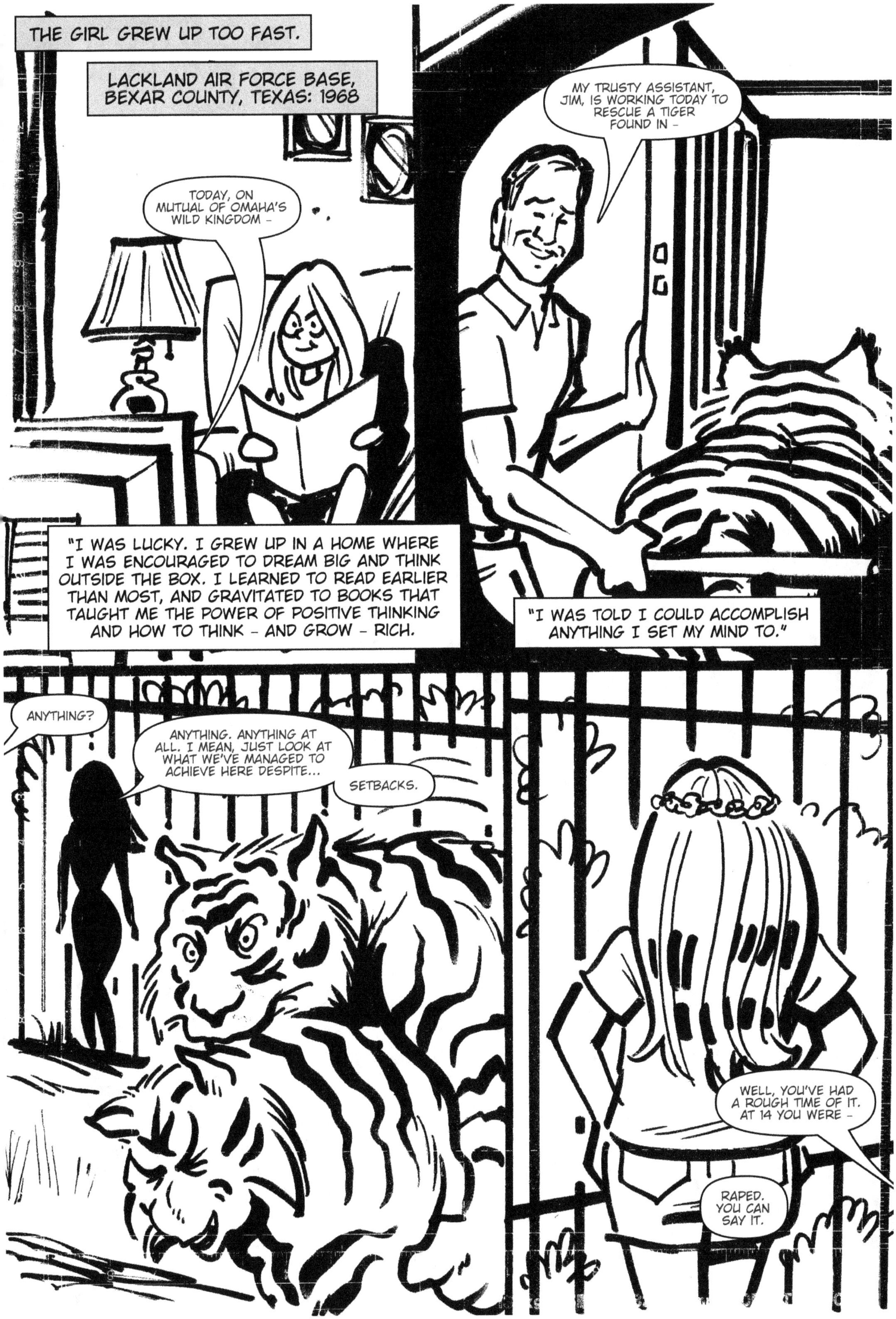
THE GIRL GREW UP TOO FAST.
LACKLAND AIR FORCE BASE, BEXAR COUNTY, TEXAS: 1968
TODAY, ON MUTUAL OF OMAHA'S WILD KINGDOM –
MY TRUSTY ASSISTANT, JIM, IS WORKING TODAY TO RESCUE A TIGER FOUND IN –
"I WAS LUCKY. I GREW UP IN A HOME WHERE I WAS ENCOURAGED TO DREAM BIG AND THINK OUTSIDE THE BOX. I LEARNED TO READ EARLIER THAN MOST, AND GRAVITATED TO BOOKS THAT TAUGHT ME THE POWER OF POSITIVE THINKING AND HOW TO THINK – AND GROW – RICH.
"I WAS TOLD I COULD ACCOMPLISH ANYTHING I SET MY MIND TO."
ANYTHING?
ANYTHING. ANYTHING AT ALL. I MEAN, JUST LOOK AT WHAT WE'VE MANAGED TO ACHIEVE HERE DESPITE...
SETBACKS.
WELL, YOU'VE HAD A ROUGH TIME OF IT. AT 14 YOU WERE –
RAPED. YOU CAN SAY IT.

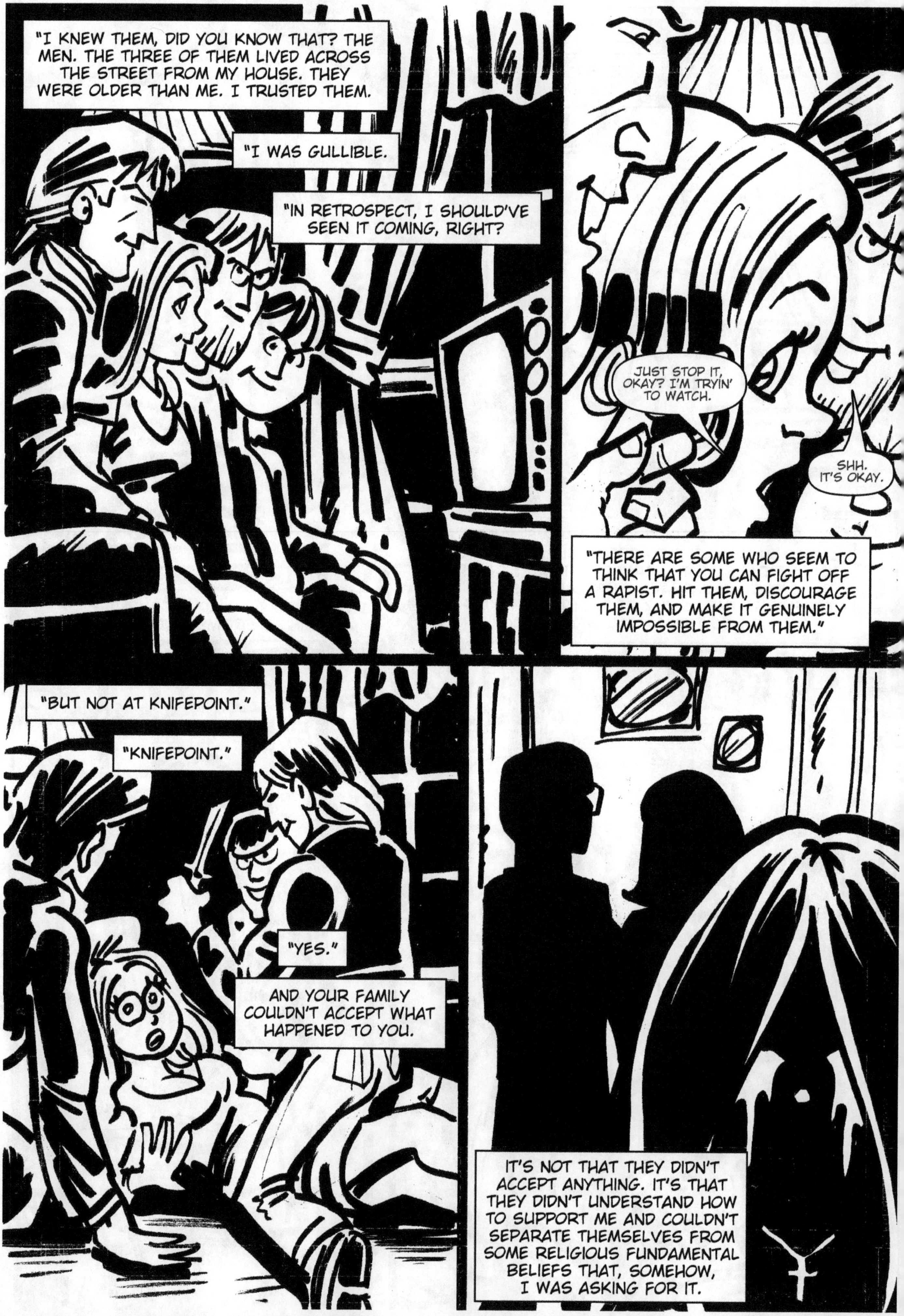
"I KNEW THEM, DID YOU KNOW THAT? THE MEN. THE THREE OF THEM LIVED ACROSS THE STREET FROM MY HOUSE. THEY WERE OLDER THAN ME. I TRUSTED THEM.
"I WAS GULLIBLE.
"IN RETROSPECT, I SHOULD'VE SEEN IT COMING, RIGHT?
JUST STOP IT, OKAY? I'M TRYIN' TO WATCH.
SHH. IT'S OKAY.
"THERE ARE SOME WHO SEEM TO THINK THAT YOU CAN FIGHT OFF A RAPIST. HIT THEM, DISCOURAGE THEM, AND MAKE IT GENUINELY IMPOSSIBLE FROM THEM."
"BUT NOT AT KNIFEPOINT."
"KNIFEPOINT."
"YES."
AND YOUR FAMILY COULDN'T ACCEPT WHAT HAPPENED TO YOU.
IT'S NOT THAT THEY DIDN'T ACCEPT ANYTHING. IT'S THAT THEY DIDN'T UNDERSTAND HOW TO SUPPORT ME AND COULDN'T SEPARATE THEMSELVES FROM SOME RELIGIOUS FUNDAMENTAL BELIEFS THAT, SOMEHOW, I WAS ASKING FOR IT.

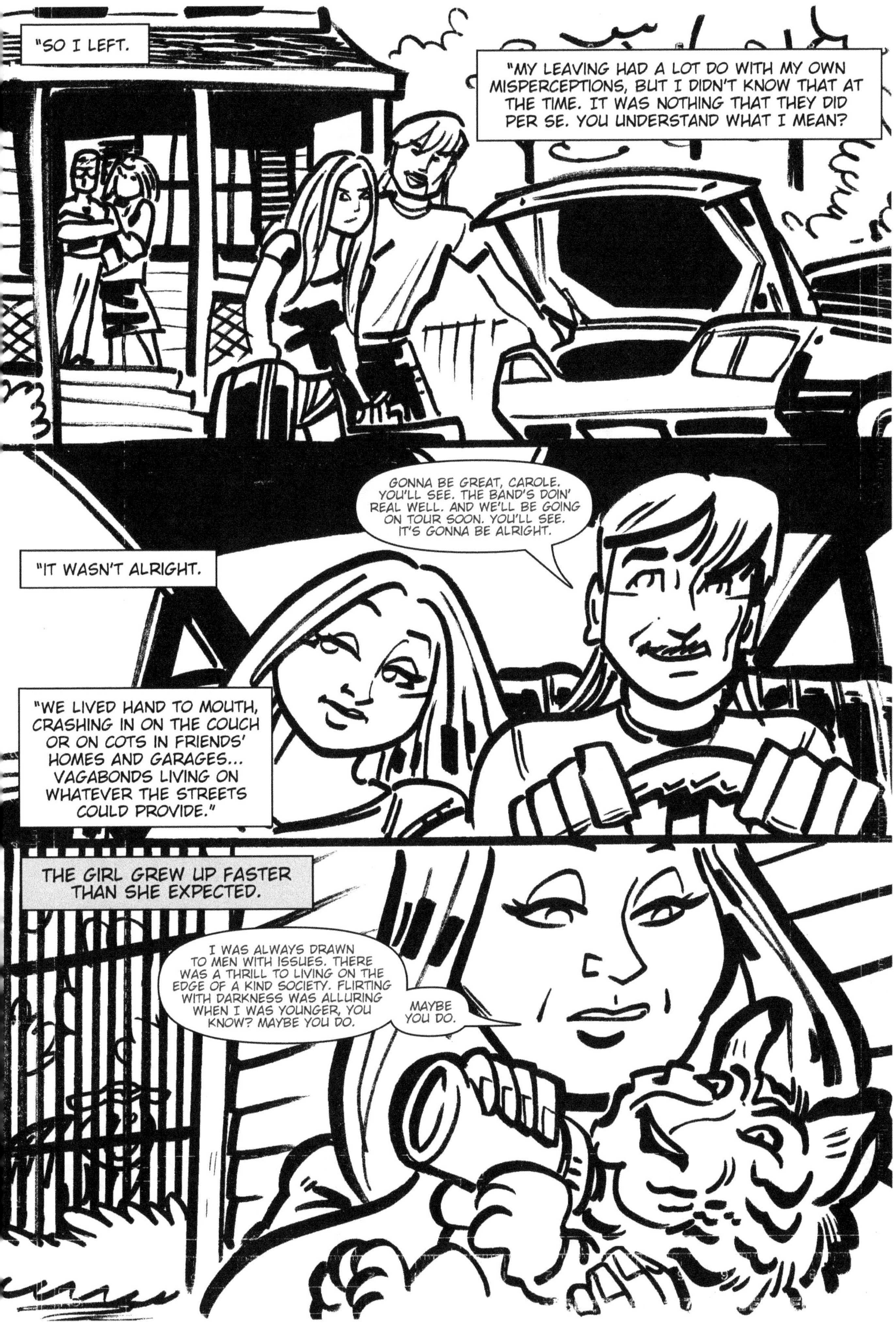
"SO I LEFT.
"MY LEAVING HAD A LOT DO WITH MY OWN MISPERCEPTIONS, BUT I DIDN'T KNOW THAT AT THE TIME. IT WAS NOTHING THAT THEY DID PER SE. YOU UNDERSTAND WHAT I MEAN?
GONNA BE GREAT, CAROLE. YOU'LL SEE. THE BAND'S DOIN' REAL WELL. AND WE'LL BE GOING ON TOUR SOON. YOU'LL SEE. IT'S GONNA BE ALRIGHT.
"IT WASN'T ALRIGHT.
"WE LIVED HAND TO MOUTH, CRASHING IN ON THE COUCH OR ON COTS IN FRIENDS' HOMES AND GARAGES... VAGABONDS LIVING ON WHATEVER THE STREETS COULD PROVIDE."
THE GIRL GREW UP FASTER THAN SHE EXPECTED.
I WAS ALWAYS DRAWN TO MEN WITH ISSUES. THERE WAS A THRILL TO LIVING ON THE EDGE OF A KIND SOCIETY. FLIRTING WITH DARKNESS WAS ALLURING WHEN I WAS YOUNGER, YOU KNOW? MAYBE YOU DO.
MAYBE YOU DO.

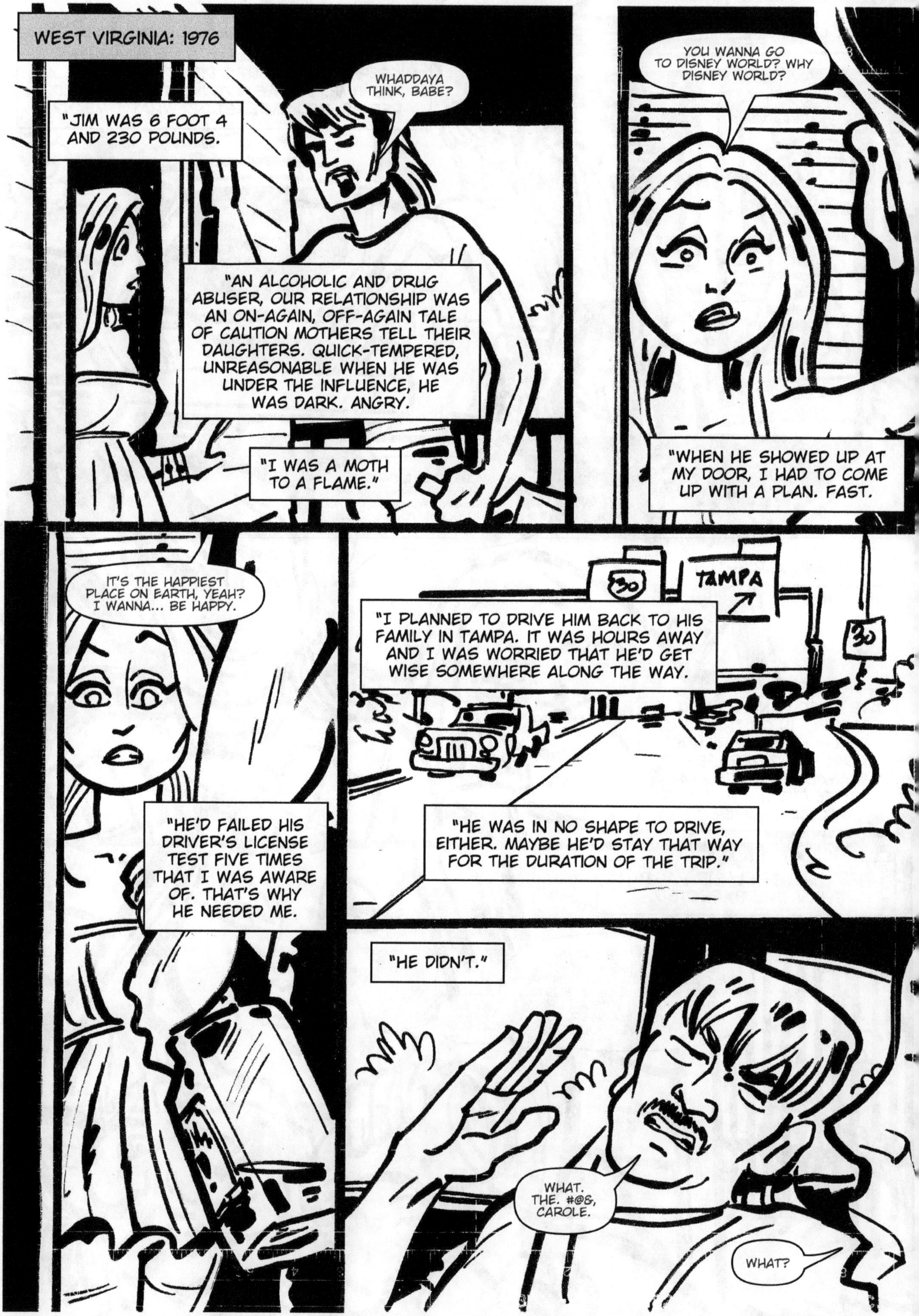
WEST VIRGINIA: 1976
"JIM WAS 6 FOOT 4 AND 230 POUNDS.
WHADDAYA THINK, BABE?
"AN ALCOHOLIC AND DRUG ABUSER, OUR RELATIONSHIP WAS AN ON-AGAIN, OFF-AGAIN TALE OF CAUTION MOTHERS TELL THEIR DAUGHTERS. QUICK-TEMPERED, UNREASONABLE WHEN HE WAS UNDER THE INFLUENCE, HE WAS DARK. ANGRY.
"I WAS A MOTH TO A FLAME."
YOU WANNA GO TO DISNEY WORLD? WHY DISNEY WORLD?
"WHEN HE SHOWED UP AT MY DOOR, I HAD TO COME UP WITH A PLAN. FAST.
IT'S THE HAPPIEST PLACE ON EARTH, YEAH? I WANNA... BE HAPPY.
"HE'D FAILED HIS DRIVER'S LICENSE TEST FIVE TIMES THAT I WAS AWARE OF. THAT'S WHY HE NEEDED ME.
TAMPA
30
30
"I PLANNED TO DRIVE HIM BACK TO HIS FAMILY IN TAMPA. IT WAS HOURS AWAY AND I WAS WORRIED THAT HE'D GET WISE SOMEWHERE ALONG THE WAY.
"HE WAS IN NO SHAPE TO DRIVE, EITHER. MAYBE HE'D STAY THAT WAY FOR THE DURATION OF THE TRIP."
"HE DIDN'T."
WHAT. THE. #@&, CAROLE.
WHAT?

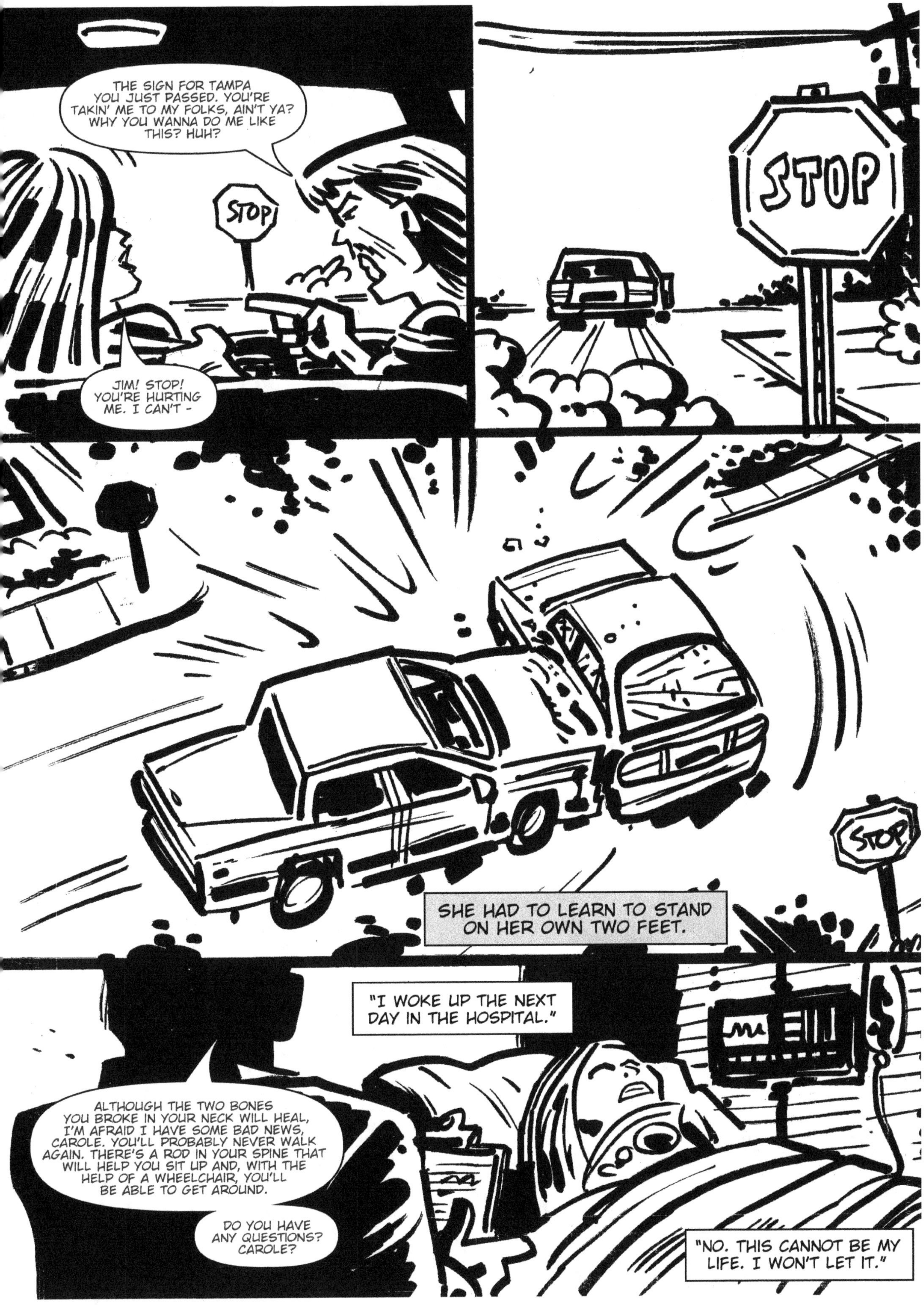
THE SIGN FOR TAMPA YOU JUST PASSED. YOU'RE TAKIN' ME TO MY FOLKS, AIN'T YA? WHY YOU WANNA DO ME LIKE THIS? HUH?
STOP
JIM! STOP! YOU'RE HURTING ME. I CAN'T -
STOP
STOP
SHE HAD TO LEARN TO STAND ON HER OWN TWO FEET.
"I WOKE UP THE NEXT DAY IN THE HOSPITAL."
ALTHOUGH THE TWO BONES YOU BROKE IN YOUR NECK WILL HEAL, I'M AFRAID I HAVE SOME BAD NEWS, CAROLE. YOU'LL PROBABLY NEVER WALK AGAIN. THERE'S A ROD IN YOUR SPINE THAT WILL HELP YOU SIT UP AND, WITH THE HELP OF A WHEELCHAIR, YOU'LL BE ABLE TO GET AROUND.
DO YOU HAVE ANY QUESTIONS? CAROLE?
"NO. THIS CANNOT BE MY LIFE. I WON'T LET IT."

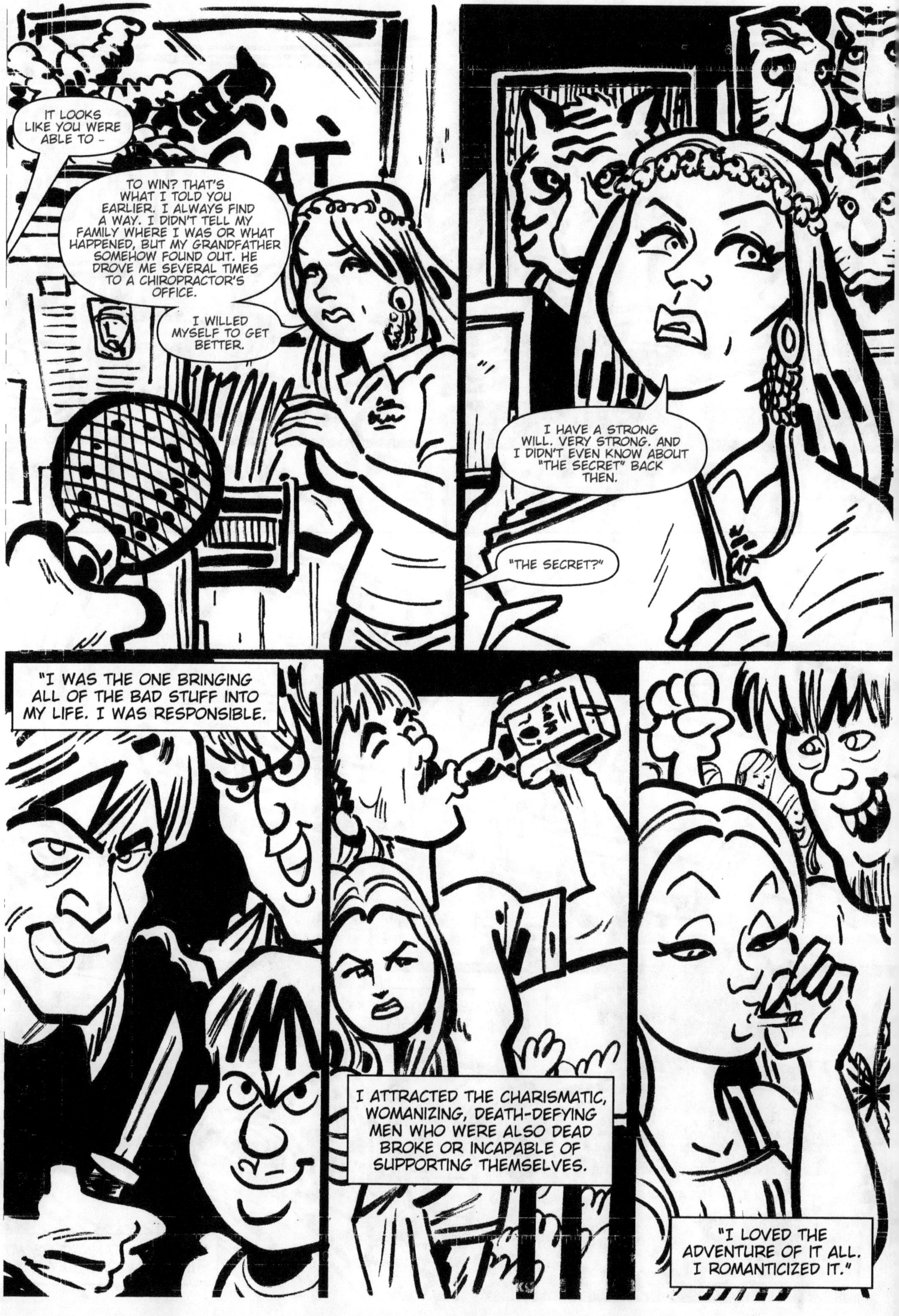

IT LOOKS LIKE YOU WERE ABLE TO –
TO WIN? THAT'S WHAT I TOLD YOU EARLIER. I ALWAYS FIND A WAY. I DIDN'T TELL MY FAMILY WHERE I WAS OR WHAT HAPPENED, BUT MY GRANDFATHER SOMEHOW FOUND OUT. HE DROVE ME SEVERAL TIMES TO A CHIROPRACTOR'S OFFICE.
I WILLED MYSELF TO GET BETTER.
CAT
I HAVE A STRONG WILL. VERY STRONG. AND I DIDN'T EVEN KNOW ABOUT "THE SECRET" BACK THEN.
"THE SECRET?"
"I WAS THE ONE BRINGING ALL OF THE BAD STUFF INTO MY LIFE. I WAS RESPONSIBLE.
I ATTRACTED THE CHARISMATIC, WOMANIZING, DEATH-DEFYING MEN WHO WERE ALSO DEAD BROKE OR INCAPABLE OF SUPPORTING THEMSELVES.
"I LOVED THE ADVENTURE OF IT ALL. I ROMANTICIZED IT."

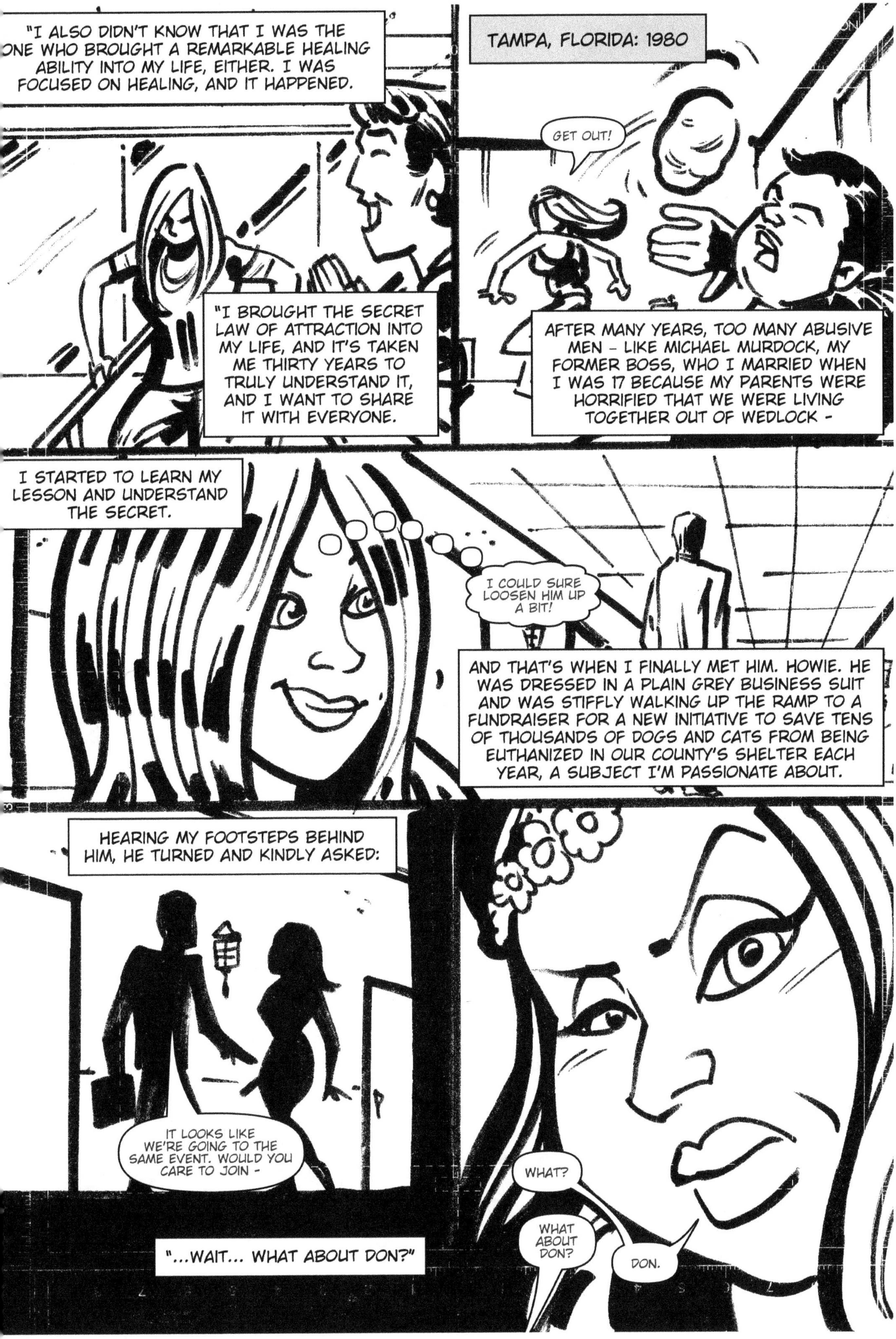
"I ALSO DIDN'T KNOW THAT I WAS THE ONE WHO BROUGHT A REMARKABLE HEALING ABILITY INTO MY LIFE, EITHER. I WAS FOCUSED ON HEALING, AND IT HAPPENED.
"I BROUGHT THE SECRET LAW OF ATTRACTION INTO MY LIFE, AND IT'S TAKEN ME THIRTY YEARS TO TRULY UNDERSTAND IT, AND I WANT TO SHARE IT WITH EVERYONE.
TAMPA, FLORIDA: 1980
GET OUT!
AFTER MANY YEARS, TOO MANY ABUSIVE MEN – LIKE MICHAEL MURDOCK, MY FORMER BOSS, WHO I MARRIED WHEN I WAS 17 BECAUSE MY PARENTS WERE HORRIFIED THAT WE WERE LIVING TOGETHER OUT OF WEDLOCK –
I STARTED TO LEARN MY LESSON AND UNDERSTAND THE SECRET.
I COULD SURE LOOSEN HIM UP A BIT!
AND THAT'S WHEN I FINALLY MET HIM. HOWIE. HE WAS DRESSED IN A PLAIN GREY BUSINESS SUIT AND WAS STIFFLY WALKING UP THE RAMP TO A FUNDRAISER FOR A NEW INITIATIVE TO SAVE TENS OF THOUSANDS OF DOGS AND CATS FROM BEING EUTHANIZED IN OUR COUNTY'S SHELTER EACH YEAR, A SUBJECT I'M PASSIONATE ABOUT.
HEARING MY FOOTSTEPS BEHIND HIM, HE TURNED AND KINDLY ASKED:
IT LOOKS LIKE WE'RE GOING TO THE SAME EVENT. WOULD YOU CARE TO JOIN –
"...WAIT... WHAT ABOUT DON?"
WHAT?
WHAT ABOUT DON?
DON.

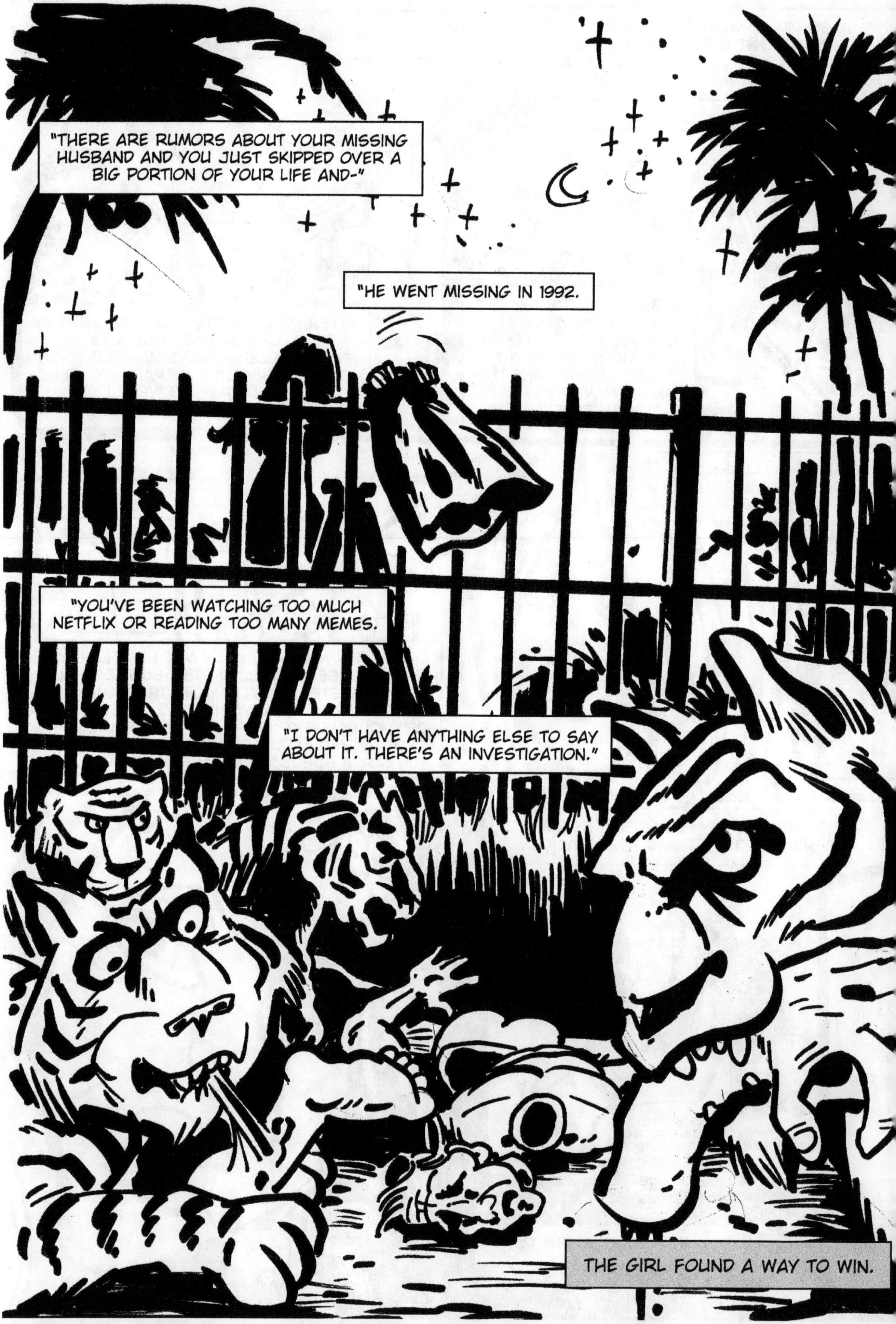
"THERE ARE RUMORS ABOUT YOUR MISSING HUSBAND AND YOU JUST SKIPPED OVER A BIG PORTION OF YOUR LIFE AND-"
"HE WENT MISSING IN 1992.
"YOU'VE BEEN WATCHING TOO MUCH NETFLIX OR READING TOO MANY MEMES.
"I DON'T HAVE ANYTHING ELSE TO SAY ABOUT IT. THERE'S AN INVESTIGATION."
THE GIRL FOUND A WAY TO WIN.

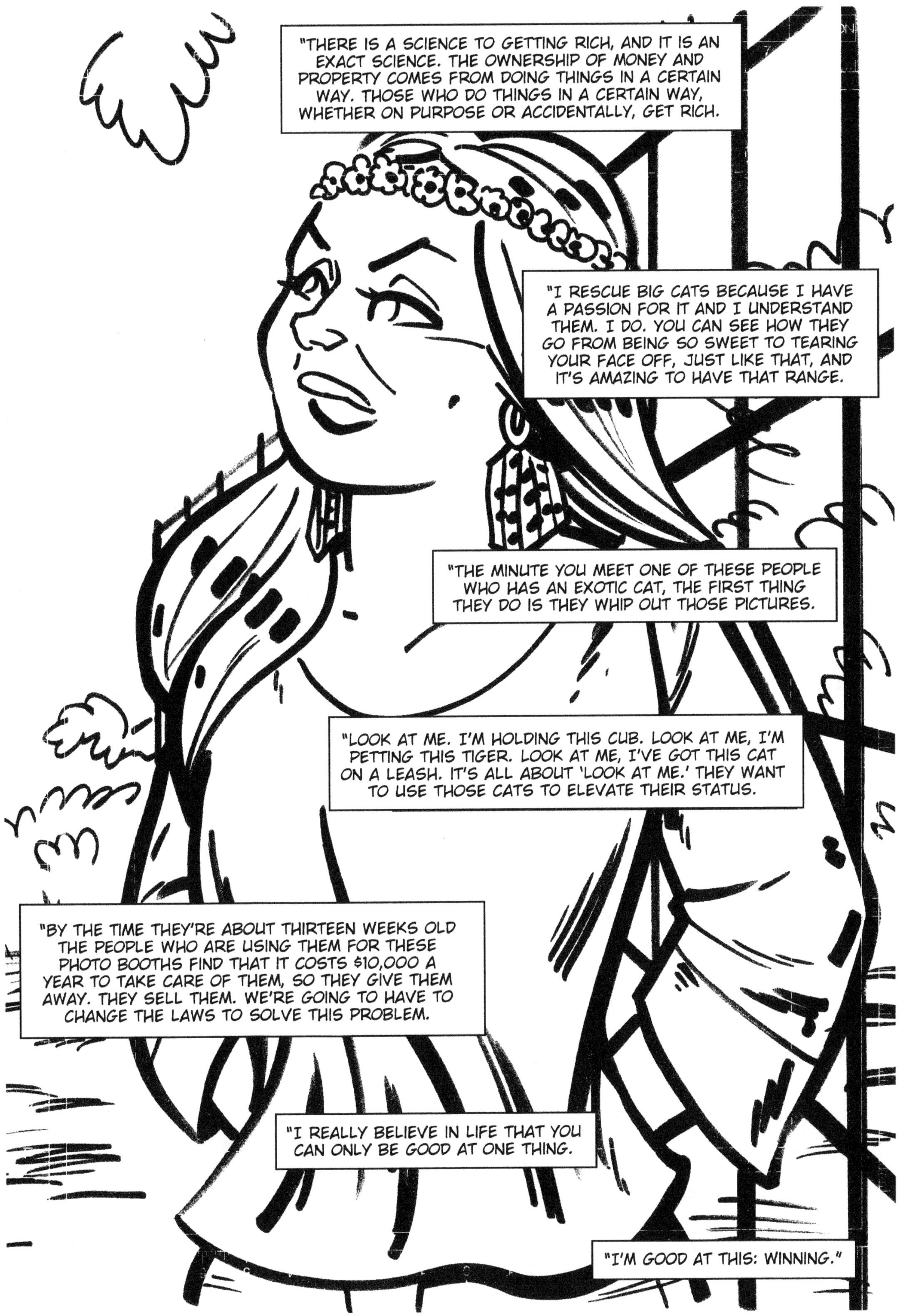
"THERE IS A SCIENCE TO GETTING RICH, AND IT IS AN EXACT SCIENCE. THE OWNERSHIP OF MONEY AND PROPERTY COMES FROM DOING THINGS IN A CERTAIN WAY. THOSE WHO DO THINGS IN A CERTAIN WAY, WHETHER ON PURPOSE OR ACCIDENTALLY, GET RICH.
"I RESCUE BIG CATS BECAUSE I HAVE A PASSION FOR IT AND I UNDERSTAND THEM. I DO. YOU CAN SEE HOW THEY GO FROM BEING SO SWEET TO TEARING YOUR FACE OFF, JUST LIKE THAT, AND IT'S AMAZING TO HAVE THAT RANGE.
"THE MINUTE YOU MEET ONE OF THESE PEOPLE WHO HAS AN EXOTIC CAT, THE FIRST THING THEY DO IS THEY WHIP OUT THOSE PICTURES.
"LOOK AT ME. I'M HOLDING THIS CUB. LOOK AT ME, I'M PETTING THIS TIGER. LOOK AT ME, I'VE GOT THIS CAT ON A LEASH. IT'S ALL ABOUT 'LOOK AT ME.' THEY WANT TO USE THOSE CATS TO ELEVATE THEIR STATUS.
"BY THE TIME THEY'RE ABOUT THIRTEEN WEEKS OLD THE PEOPLE WHO ARE USING THEM FOR THESE PHOTO BOOTHS FIND THAT IT COSTS $10,000 A YEAR TO TAKE CARE OF THEM, SO THEY GIVE THEM AWAY. THEY SELL THEM. WE'RE GOING TO HAVE TO CHANGE THE LAWS TO SOLVE THIS PROBLEM.
"I REALLY BELIEVE IN LIFE THAT YOU CAN ONLY BE GOOD AT ONE THING.
"I'M GOOD AT THIS: WINNING."

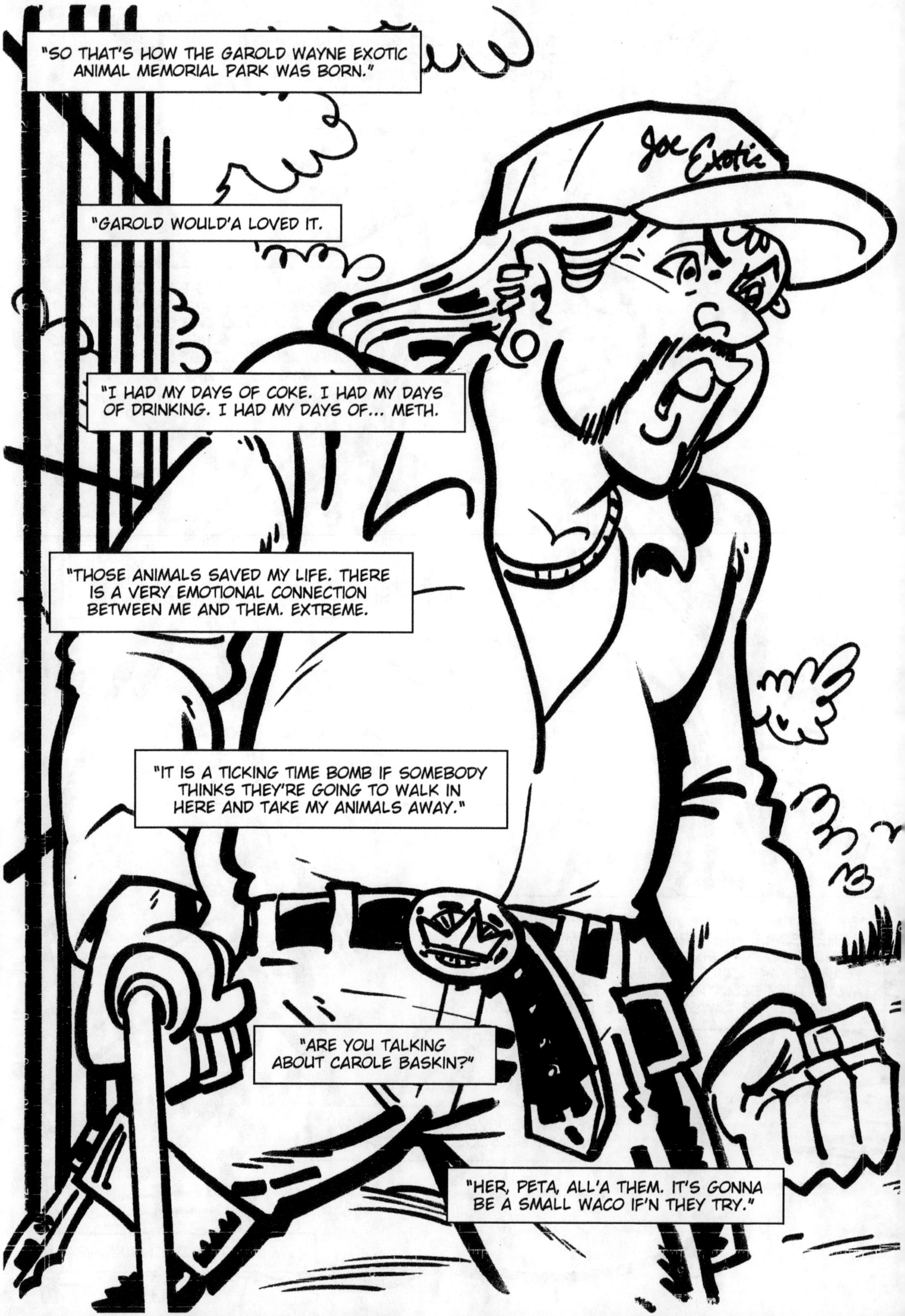
"SO THAT'S HOW THE GAROLD WAYNE EXOTIC ANIMAL MEMORIAL PARK WAS BORN."
"GAROLD WOULD'A LOVED IT.
"I HAD MY DAYS OF COKE. I HAD MY DAYS OF DRINKING. I HAD MY DAYS OF... METH.
"THOSE ANIMALS SAVED MY LIFE. THERE IS A VERY EMOTIONAL CONNECTION BETWEEN ME AND THEM. EXTREME.
"IT IS A TICKING TIME BOMB IF SOMEBODY THINKS THEY'RE GOING TO WALK IN HERE AND TAKE MY ANIMALS AWAY."
"ARE YOU TALKING ABOUT CAROLE BASKIN?"
"HER, PETA, ALL'A THEM. IT'S GONNA BE A SMALL WACO IF'N THEY TRY."
Joe Exotic

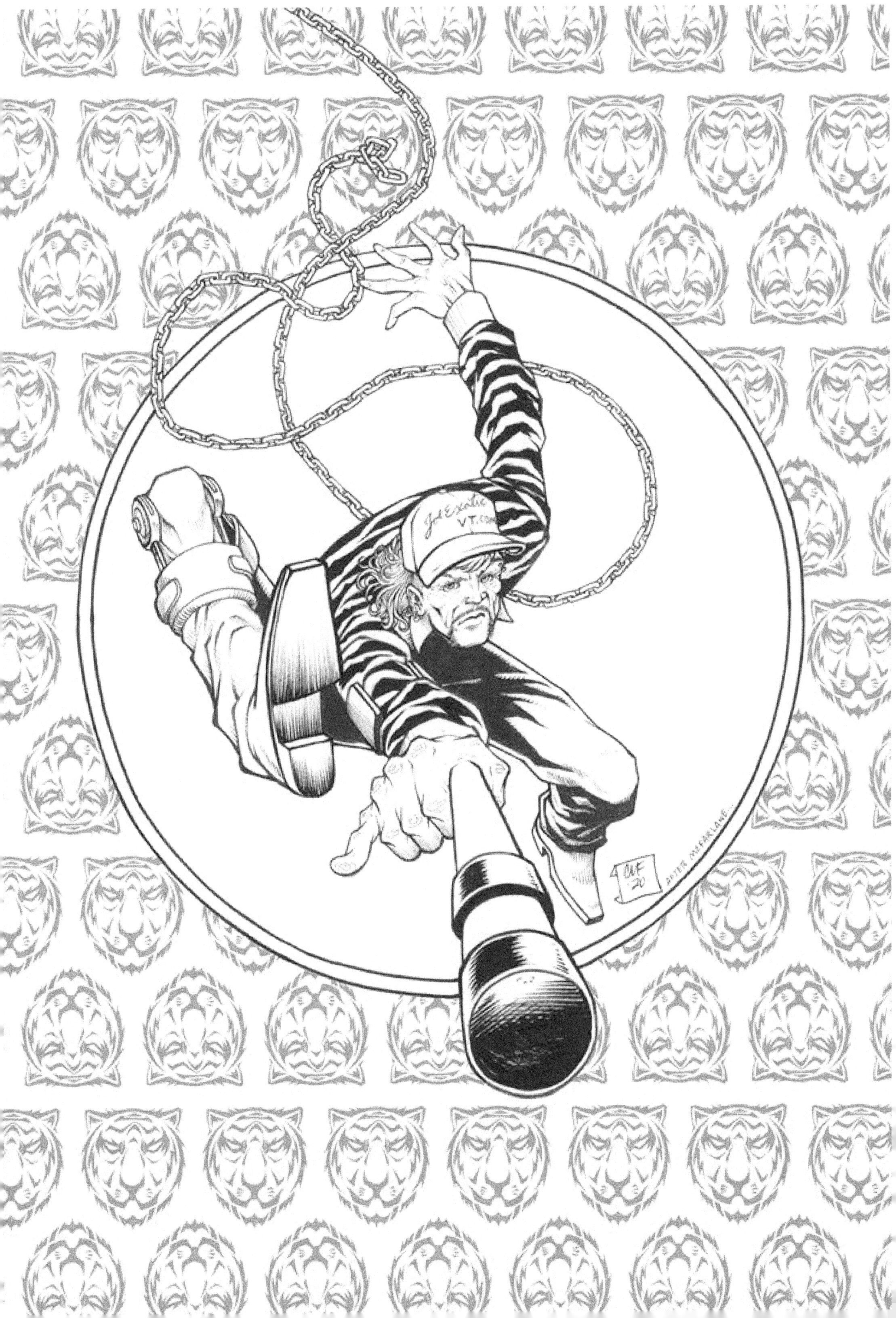
Joe Exotic
CWF '20
AFTER McFARLANE...

Joe Exotic left you
a **SECRET MESSAGE!**
Can you find it?

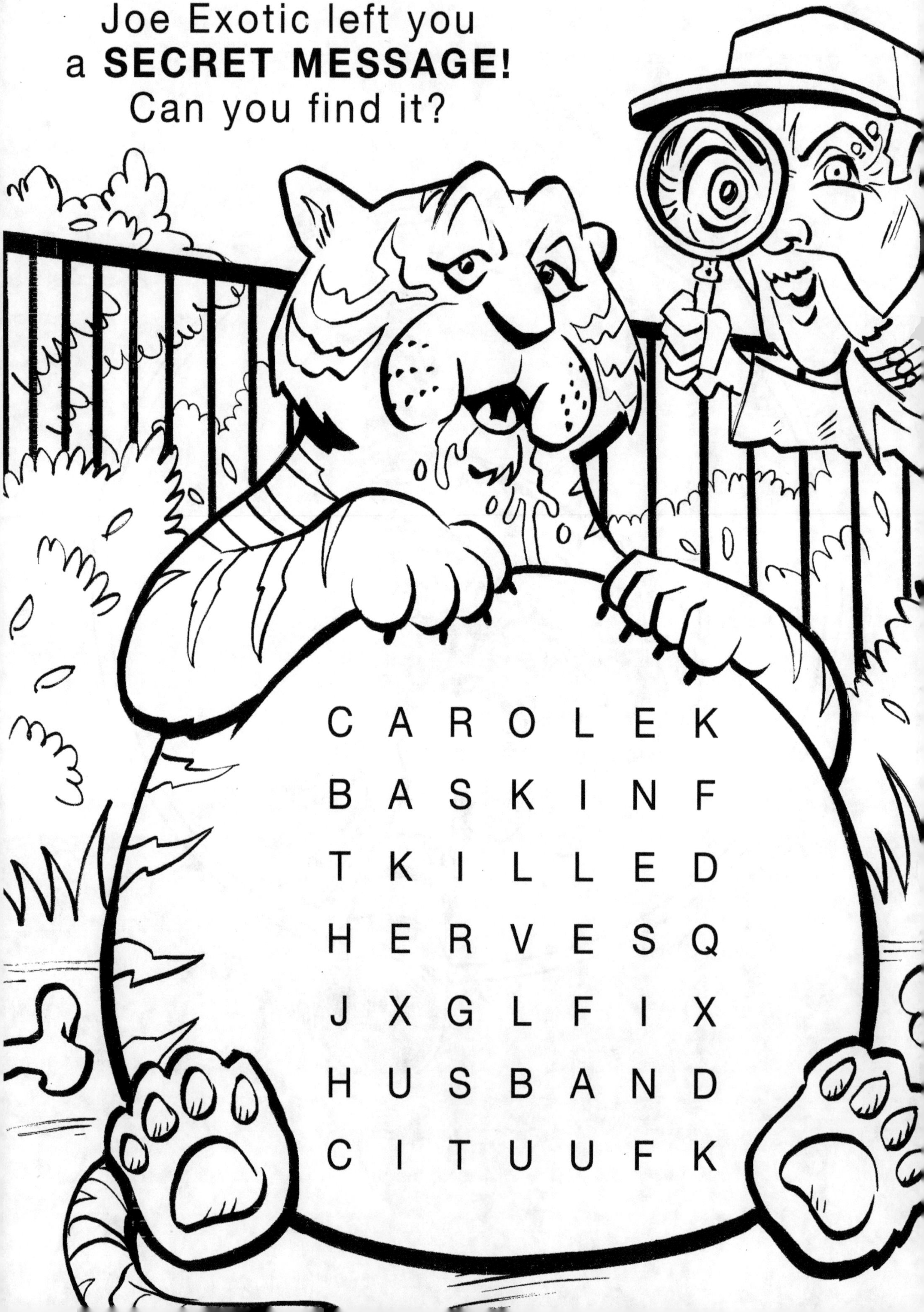
C A R O L E K
B A S K I N F
T K I L L E D
H E R V E S Q
J X G L F I X
H U S B A N D
C I T U U F K

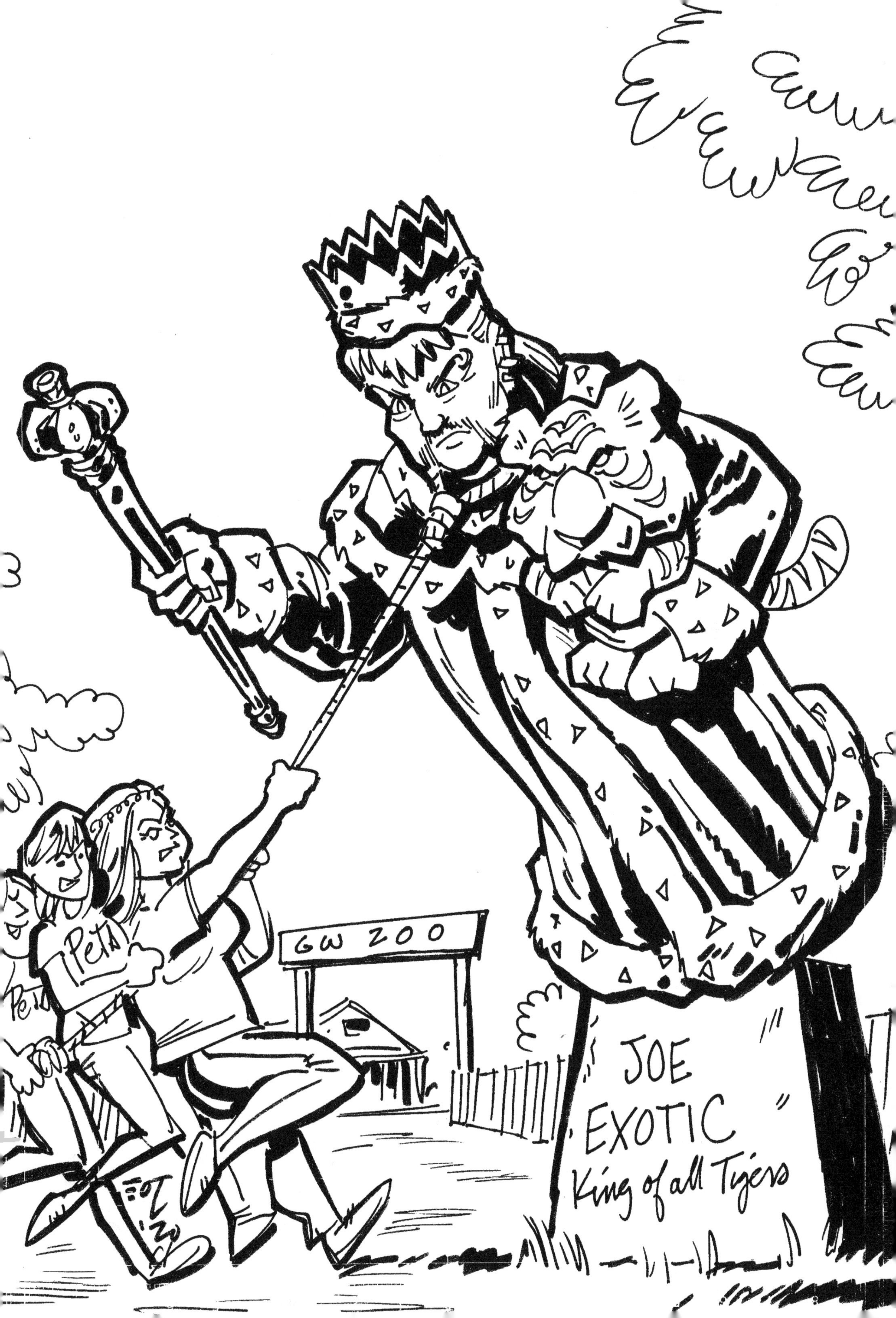
GW ZOO
PETA
JOE
"EXOTIC"
King of all Tygers

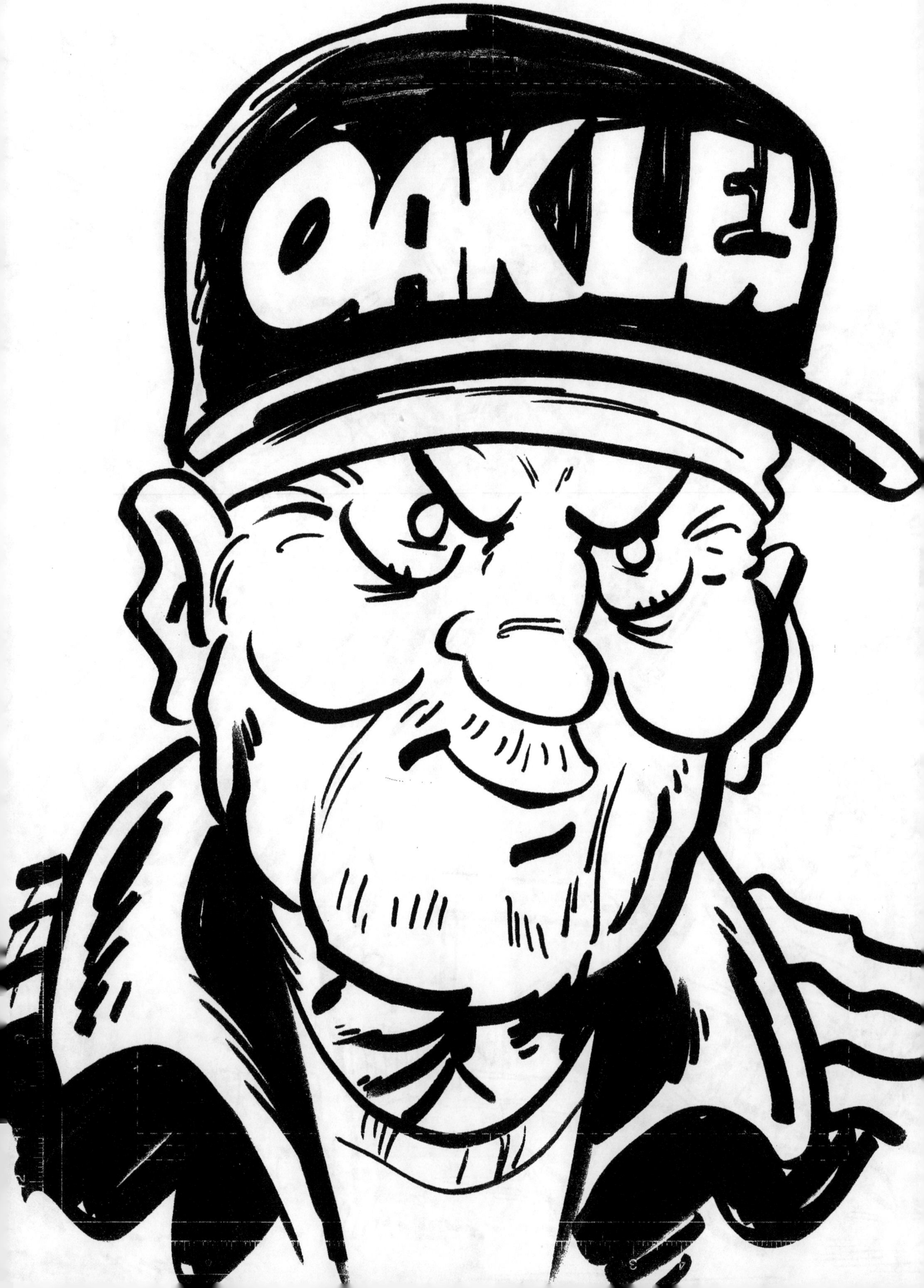
OAKLE

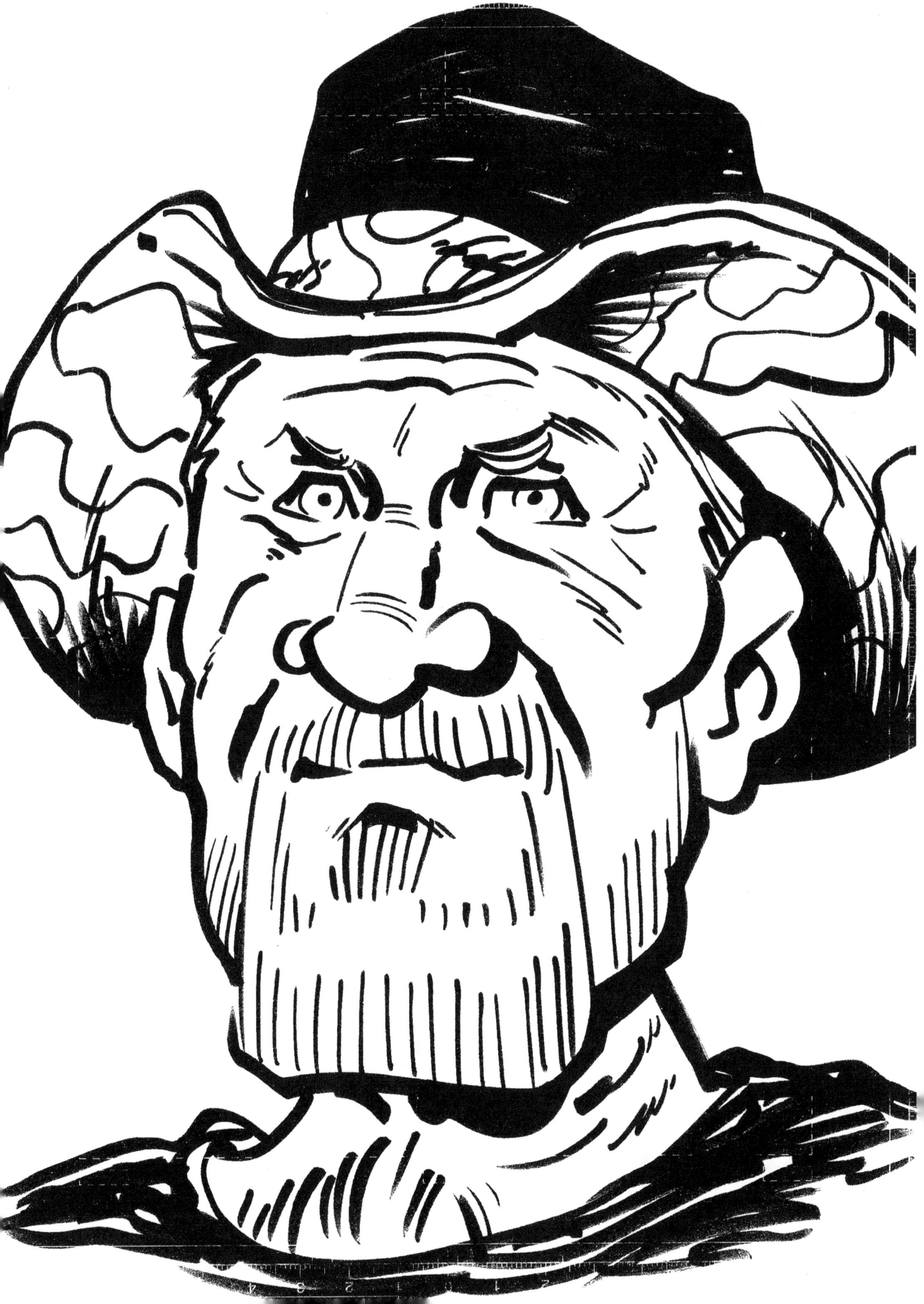

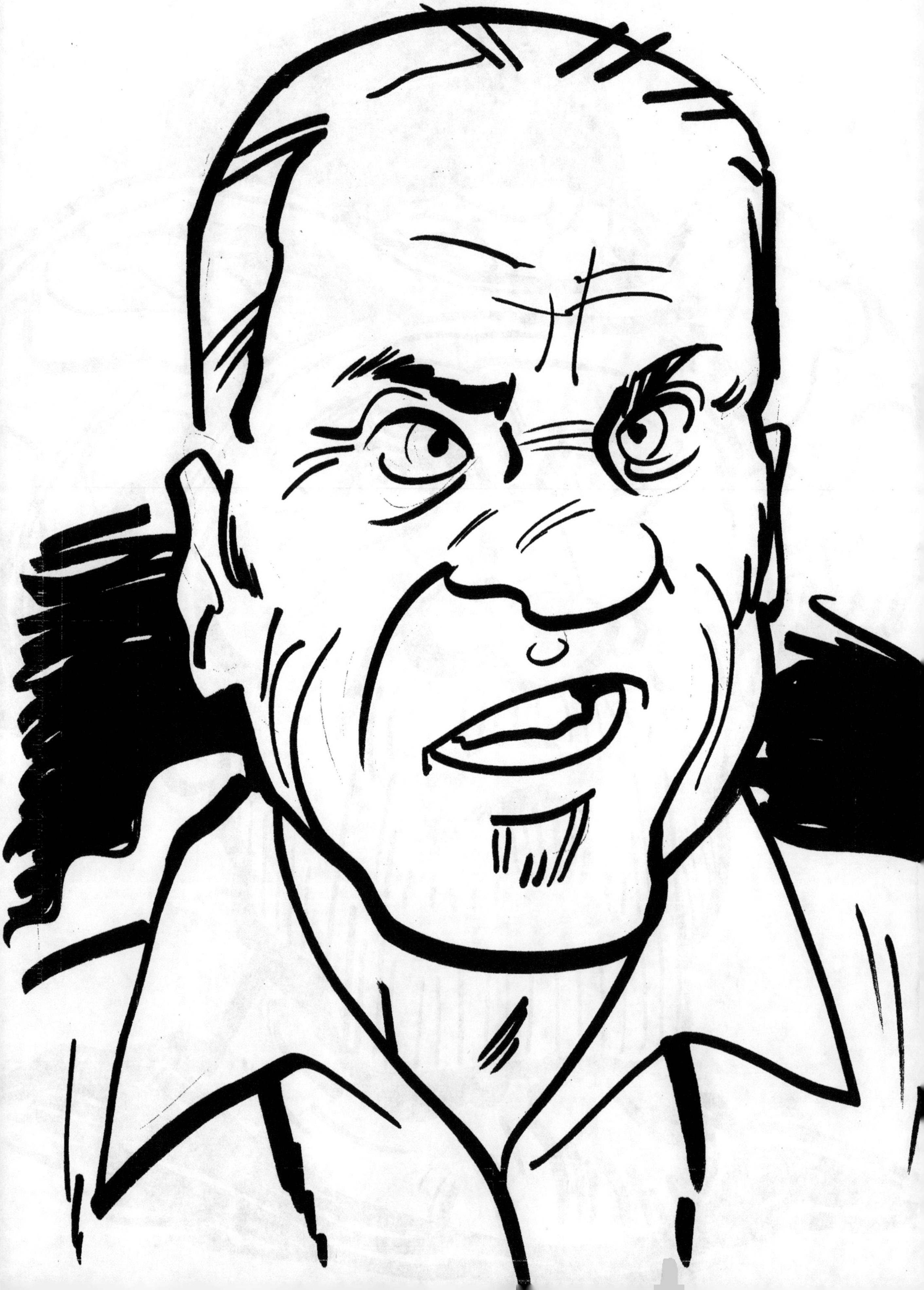

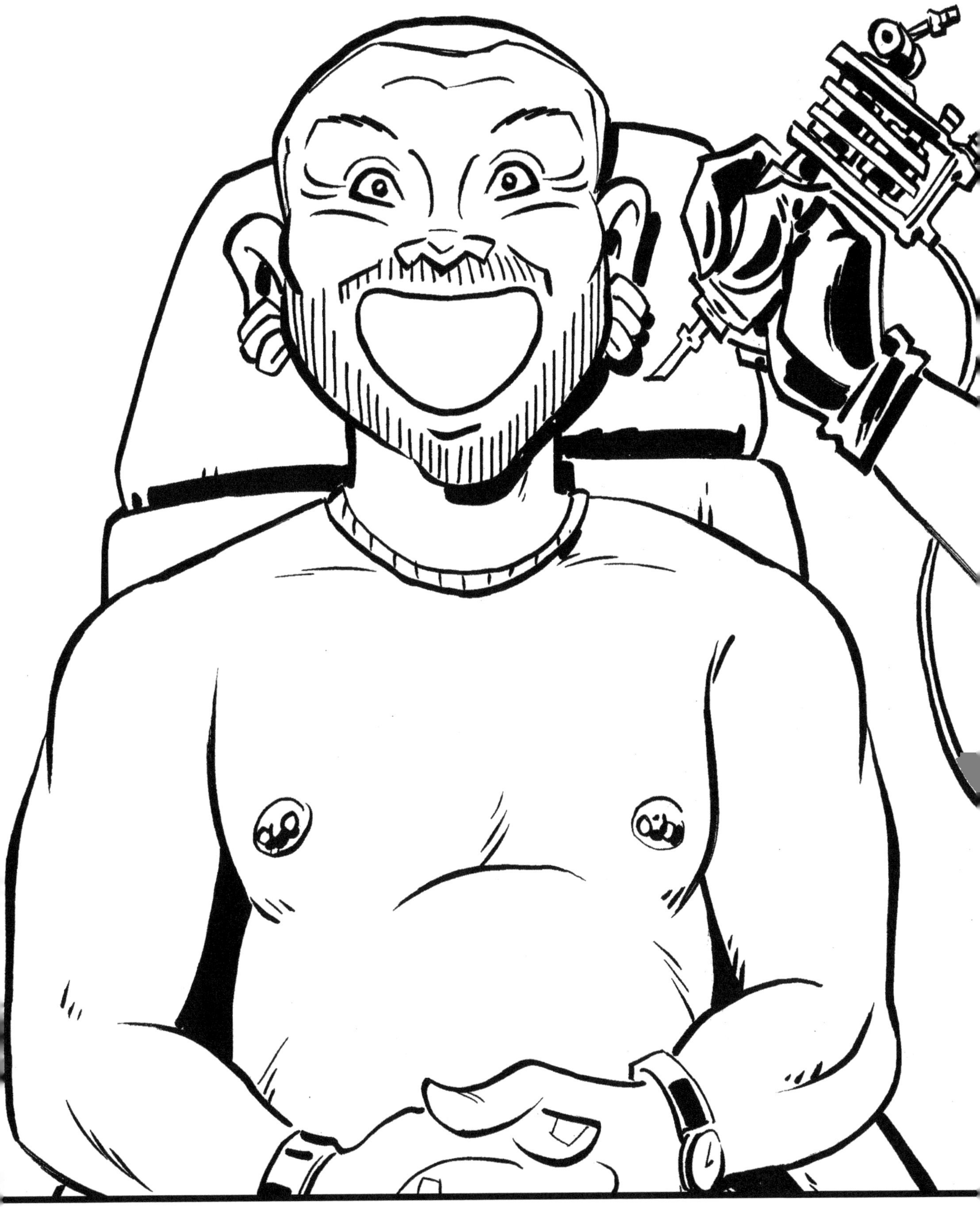

You can draw new teeth & tatts for John Finlay -
Get Creative!

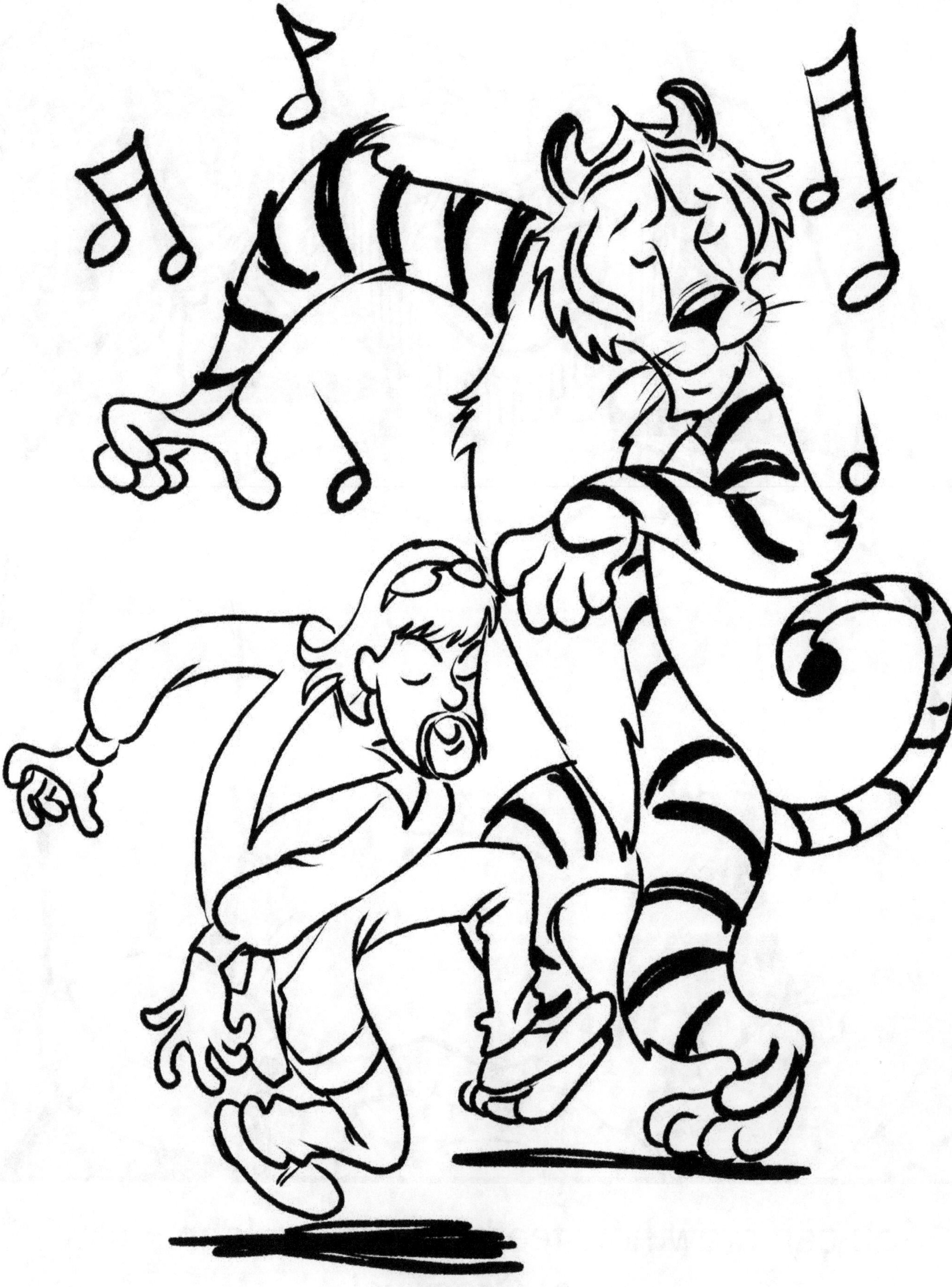

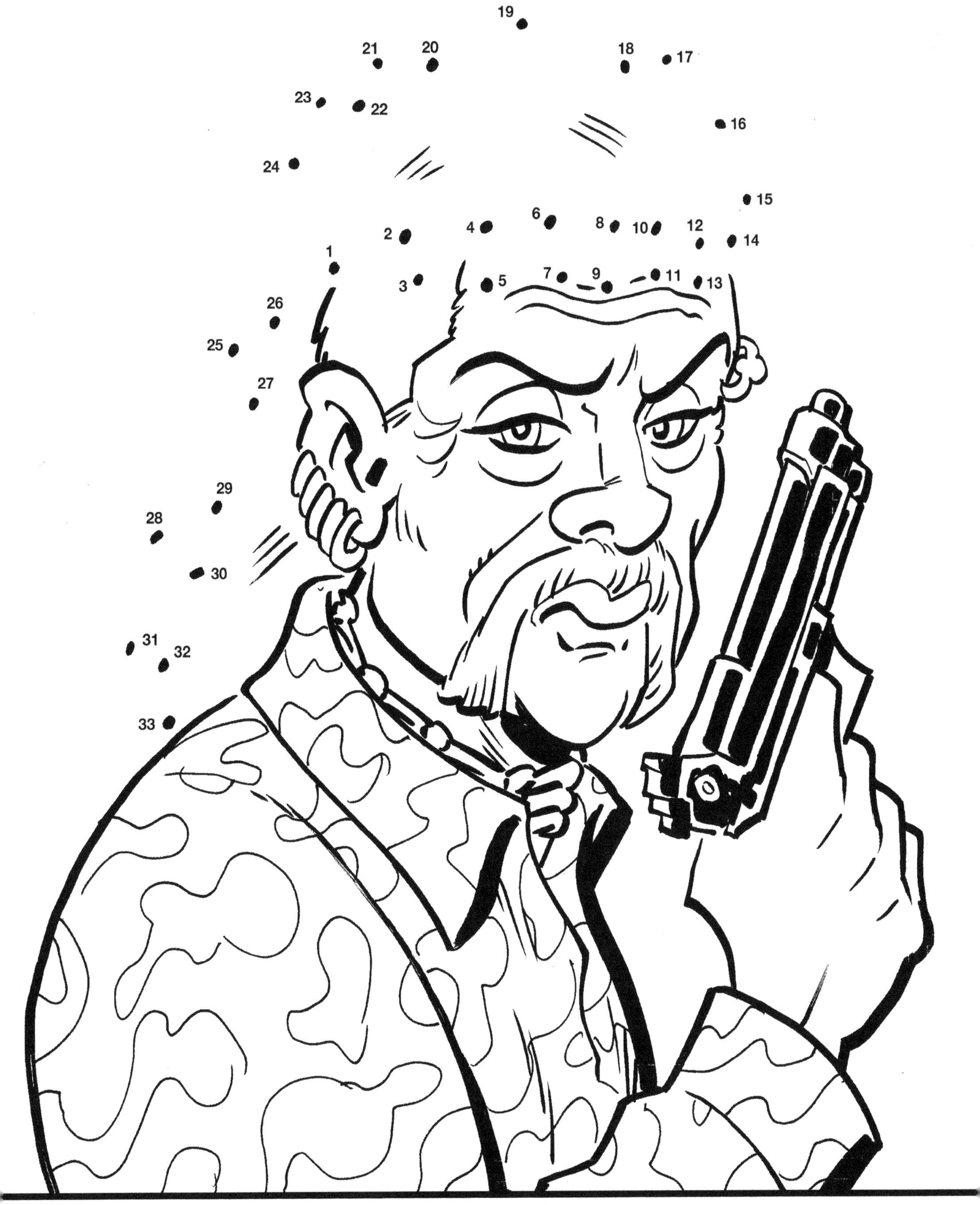
1
2
3
4
5
6
7
8
9
10
11
12
13
14
15
16
17
18
19
20
21
22
23
24
25
26
27
28
29
30
31
32
33

Connect the Mullet dots!

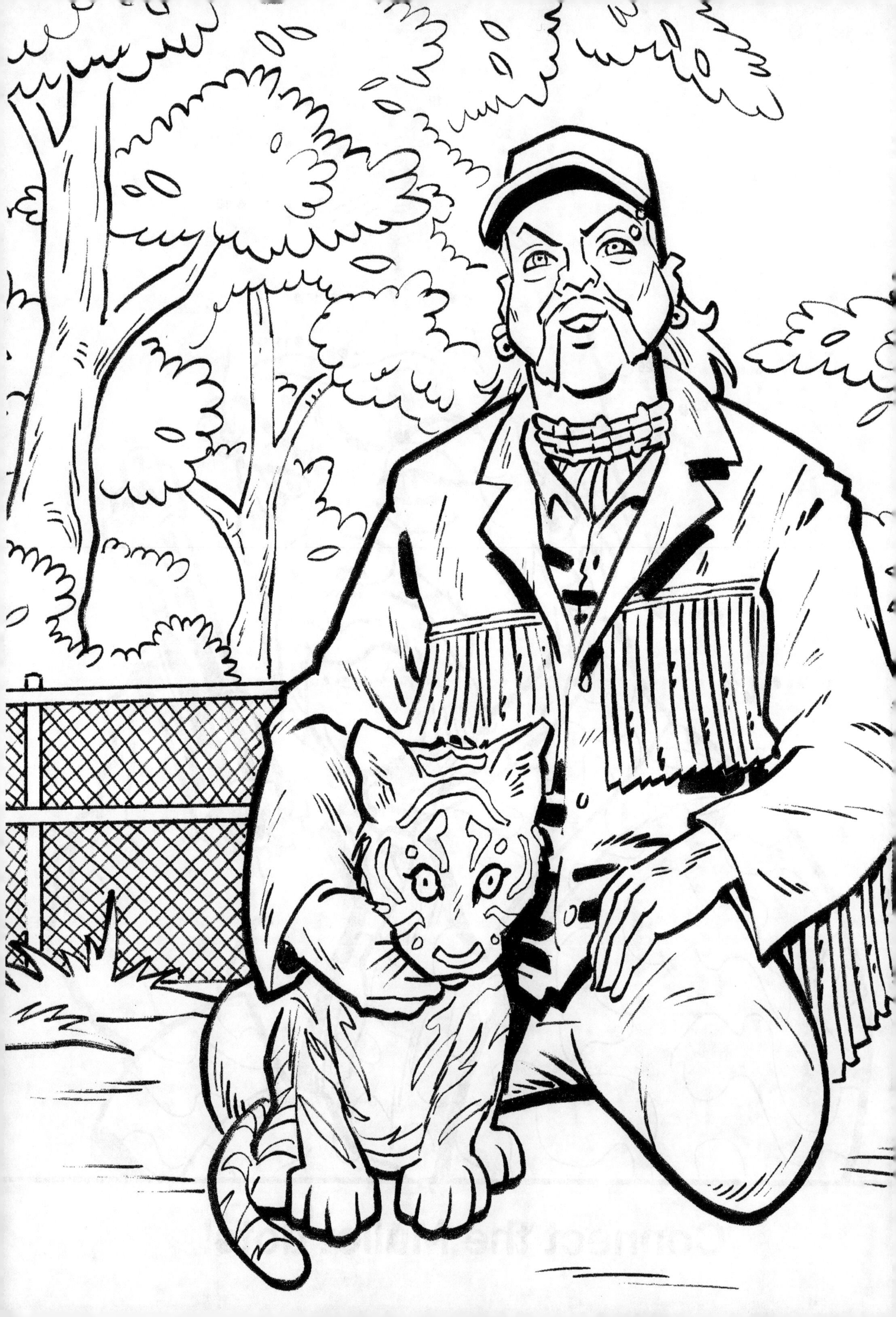

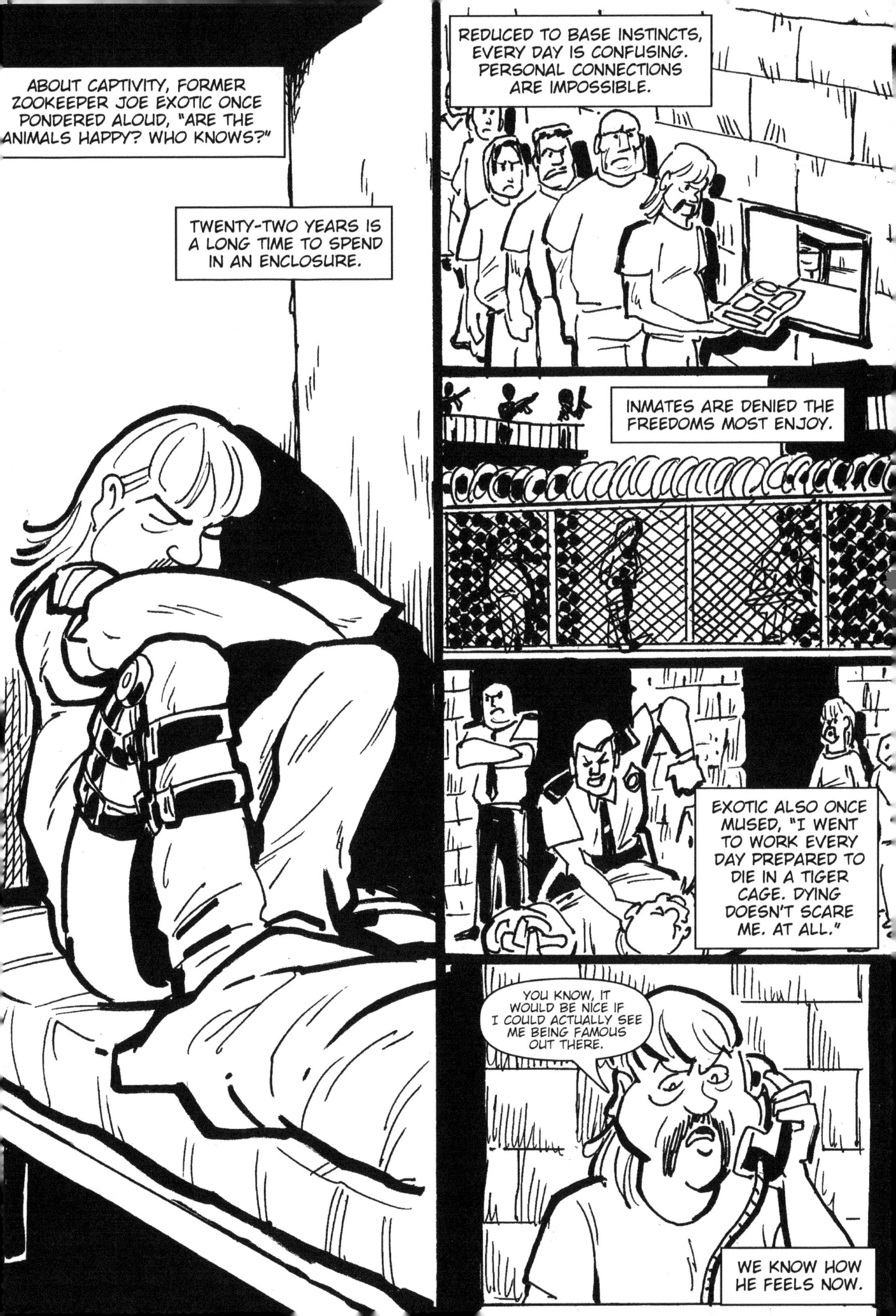
ABOUT CAPTIVITY, FORMER ZOOKEEPER JOE EXOTIC ONCE PONDERED ALOUD, "ARE THE ANIMALS HAPPY? WHO KNOWS?"
TWENTY-TWO YEARS IS A LONG TIME TO SPEND IN AN ENCLOSURE.
REDUCED TO BASE INSTINCTS, EVERY DAY IS CONFUSING. PERSONAL CONNECTIONS ARE IMPOSSIBLE.
INMATES ARE DENIED THE FREEDOMS MOST ENJOY.
EXOTIC ALSO ONCE MUSED, "I WENT TO WORK EVERY DAY PREPARED TO DIE IN A TIGER CAGE. DYING DOESN'T SCARE ME. AT ALL."
YOU KNOW, IT WOULD BE NICE IF I COULD ACTUALLY SEE ME BEING FAMOUS OUT THERE.
WE KNOW HOW HE FEELS NOW.

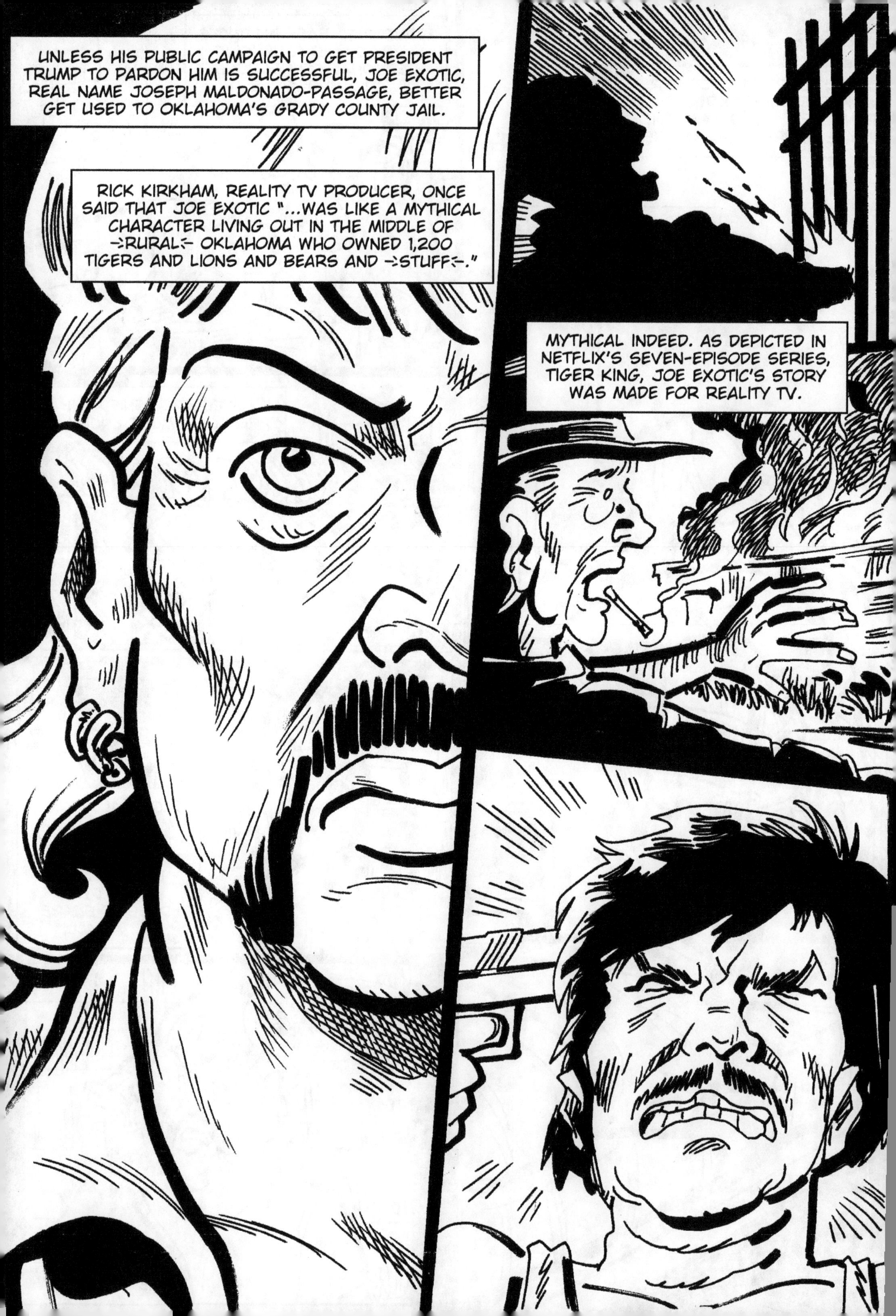
UNLESS HIS PUBLIC CAMPAIGN TO GET PRESIDENT TRUMP TO PARDON HIM IS SUCCESSFUL, JOE EXOTIC, REAL NAME JOSEPH MALDONADO-PASSAGE, BETTER GET USED TO OKLAHOMA'S GRADY COUNTY JAIL.
RICK KIRKHAM, REALITY TV PRODUCER, ONCE SAID THAT JOE EXOTIC "...WAS LIKE A MYTHICAL CHARACTER LIVING OUT IN THE MIDDLE OF ->RURAL<- OKLAHOMA WHO OWNED 1,200 TIGERS AND LIONS AND BEARS AND ->STUFF<-."
MYTHICAL INDEED. AS DEPICTED IN NETFLIX'S SEVEN-EPISODE SERIES, TIGER KING, JOE EXOTIC'S STORY WAS MADE FOR REALITY TV.

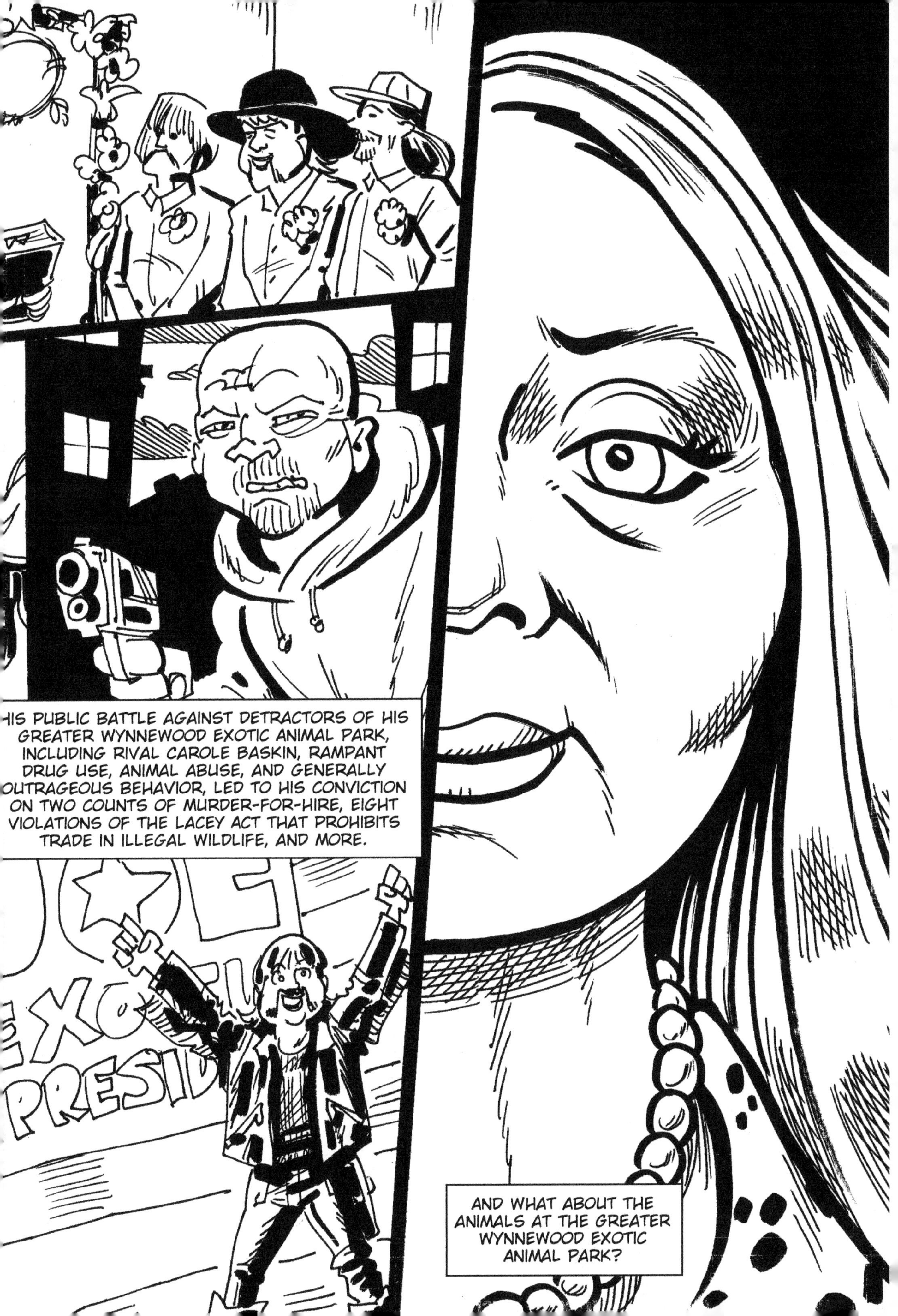
HIS PUBLIC BATTLE AGAINST DETRACTORS OF HIS GREATER WYNNEWOOD EXOTIC ANIMAL PARK, INCLUDING RIVAL CAROLE BASKIN, RAMPANT DRUG USE, ANIMAL ABUSE, AND GENERALLY OUTRAGEOUS BEHAVIOR, LED TO HIS CONVICTION ON TWO COUNTS OF MURDER-FOR-HIRE, EIGHT VIOLATIONS OF THE LACEY ACT THAT PROHIBITS TRADE IN ILLEGAL WILDLIFE, AND MORE.
AND WHAT ABOUT THE ANIMALS AT THE GREATER WYNNEWOOD EXOTIC ANIMAL PARK?

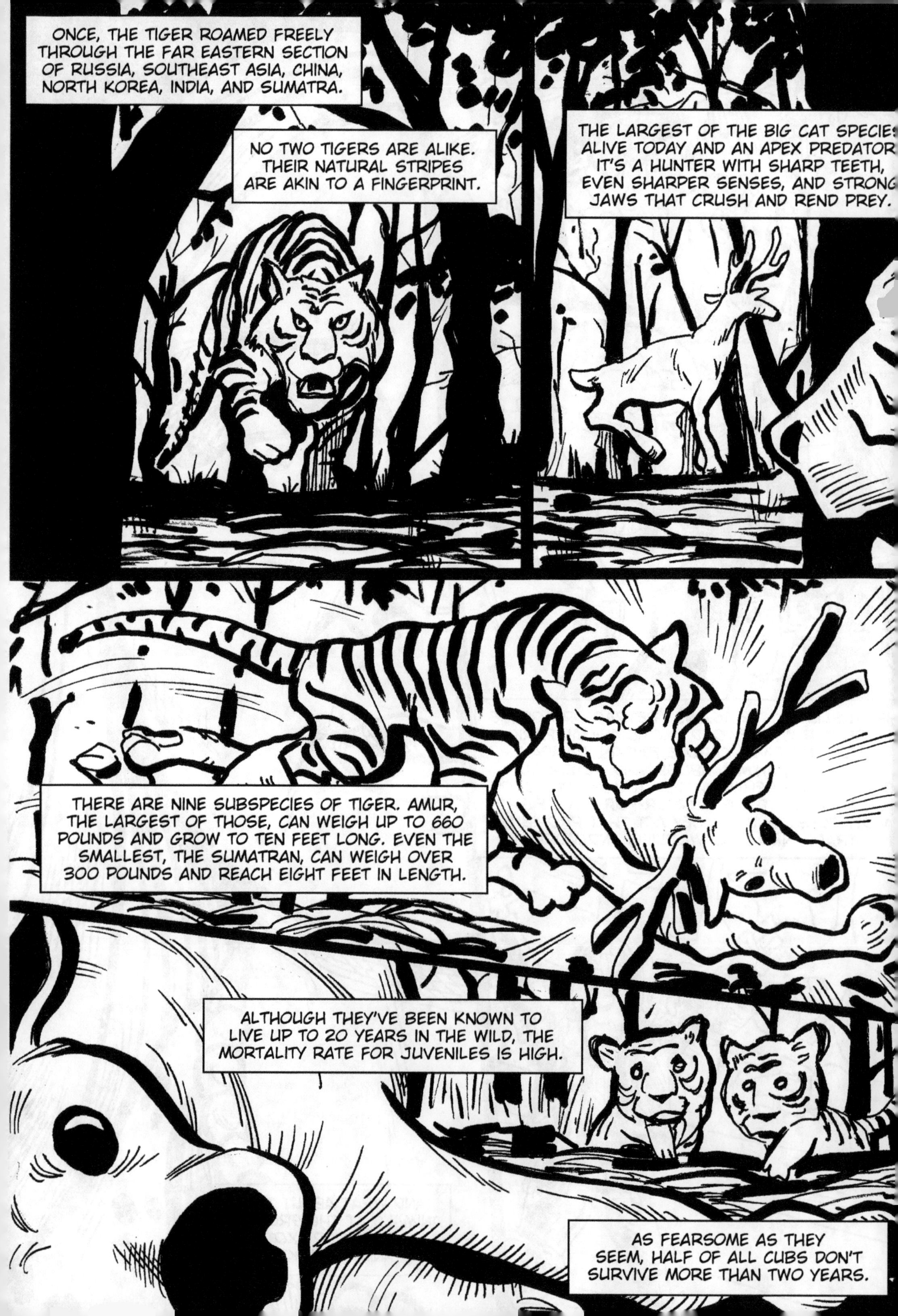
ONCE, THE TIGER ROAMED FREELY THROUGH THE FAR EASTERN SECTION OF RUSSIA, SOUTHEAST ASIA, CHINA, NORTH KOREA, INDIA, AND SUMATRA.
NO TWO TIGERS ARE ALIKE. THEIR NATURAL STRIPES ARE AKIN TO A FINGERPRINT.
THE LARGEST OF THE BIG CAT SPECIES ALIVE TODAY AND AN APEX PREDATOR, IT'S A HUNTER WITH SHARP TEETH, EVEN SHARPER SENSES, AND STRONG JAWS THAT CRUSH AND REND PREY.
THERE ARE NINE SUBSPECIES OF TIGER. AMUR, THE LARGEST OF THOSE, CAN WEIGH UP TO 660 POUNDS AND GROW TO TEN FEET LONG. EVEN THE SMALLEST, THE SUMATRAN, CAN WEIGH OVER 300 POUNDS AND REACH EIGHT FEET IN LENGTH.
ALTHOUGH THEY'VE BEEN KNOWN TO LIVE UP TO 20 YEARS IN THE WILD, THE MORTALITY RATE FOR JUVENILES IS HIGH.
AS FEARSOME AS THEY SEEM, HALF OF ALL CUBS DON'T SURVIVE MORE THAN TWO YEARS.

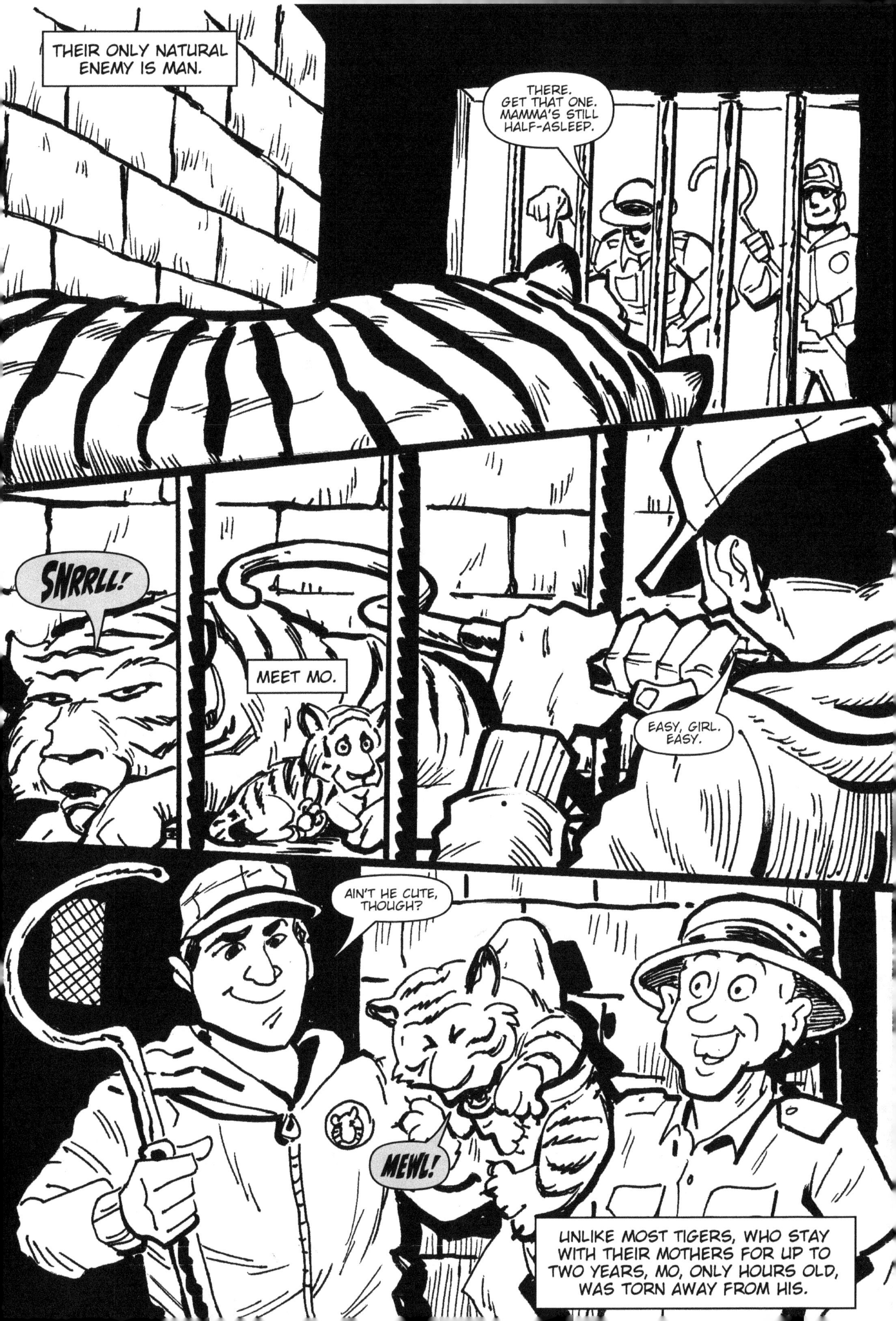
THEIR ONLY NATURAL ENEMY IS MAN.
THERE. GET THAT ONE. MAMMA'S STILL HALF-ASLEEP.
SNRRLL!
MEET MO.
EASY, GIRL. EASY.
AIN'T HE CUTE, THOUGH?
MEWL!
UNLIKE MOST TIGERS, WHO STAY WITH THEIR MOTHERS FOR UP TO TWO YEARS, MO, ONLY HOURS OLD, WAS TORN AWAY FROM HIS.

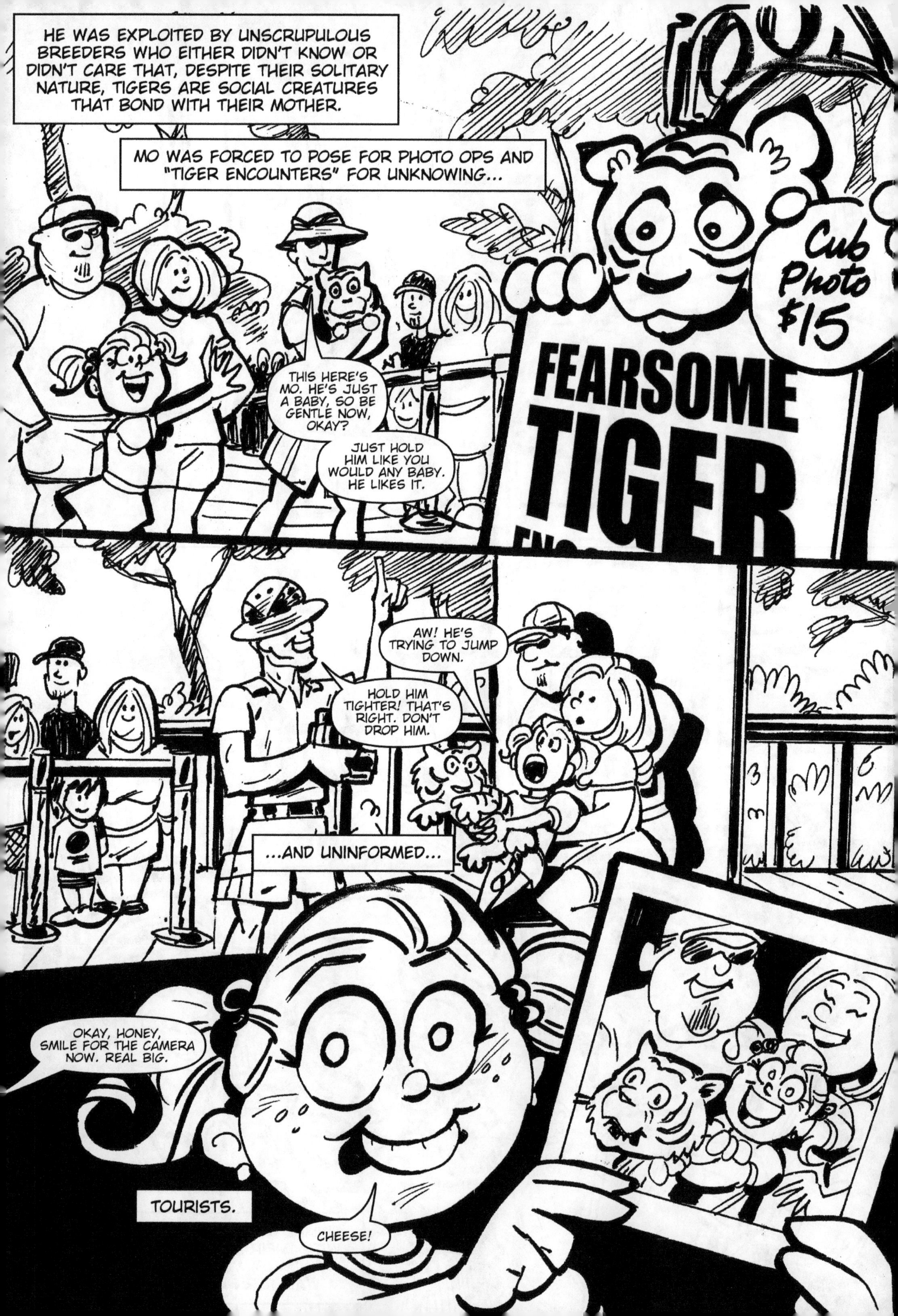
HE WAS EXPLOITED BY UNSCRUPULOUS BREEDERS WHO EITHER DIDN'T KNOW OR DIDN'T CARE THAT, DESPITE THEIR SOLITARY NATURE, TIGERS ARE SOCIAL CREATURES THAT BOND WITH THEIR MOTHER.
MO WAS FORCED TO POSE FOR PHOTO OPS AND "TIGER ENCOUNTERS" FOR UNKNOWING...
Cub Photo $15
FEARSOME TIGER
THIS HERE'S MO. HE'S JUST A BABY, SO BE GENTLE NOW, OKAY?
JUST HOLD HIM LIKE YOU WOULD ANY BABY. HE LIKES IT.
AW! HE'S TRYING TO JUMP DOWN.
HOLD HIM TIGHTER! THAT'S RIGHT. DON'T DROP HIM.
...AND UNINFORMED...
OKAY, HONEY, SMILE FOR THE CAMERA NOW. REAL BIG.
TOURISTS.
CHEESE!

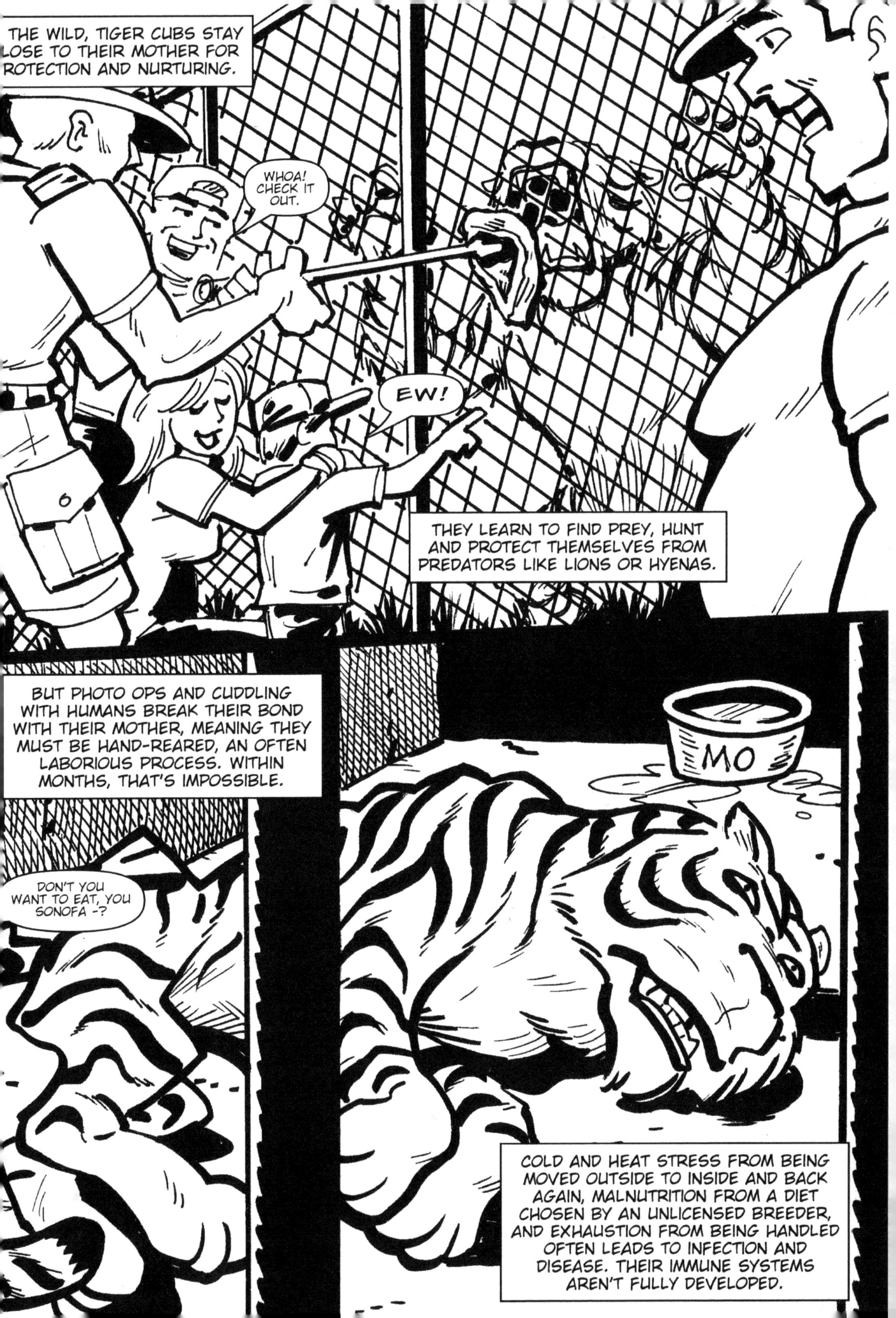
THE WILD, TIGER CUBS STAY
LOSE TO THEIR MOTHER FOR
ROTECTION AND NURTURING.
WHOA! CHECK IT OUT.
EW!
THEY LEARN TO FIND PREY, HUNT AND PROTECT THEMSELVES FROM PREDATORS LIKE LIONS OR HYENAS.
BUT PHOTO OPS AND CUDDLING WITH HUMANS BREAK THEIR BOND WITH THEIR MOTHER, MEANING THEY MUST BE HAND-REARED, AN OFTEN LABORIOUS PROCESS. WITHIN MONTHS, THAT'S IMPOSSIBLE.
DON'T YOU WANT TO EAT, YOU SONOFA -?
MO
COLD AND HEAT STRESS FROM BEING MOVED OUTSIDE TO INSIDE AND BACK AGAIN, MALNUTRITION FROM A DIET CHOSEN BY AN UNLICENSED BREEDER, AND EXHAUSTION FROM BEING HANDLED OFTEN LEADS TO INFECTION AND DISEASE. THEIR IMMUNE SYSTEMS AREN'T FULLY DEVELOPED.

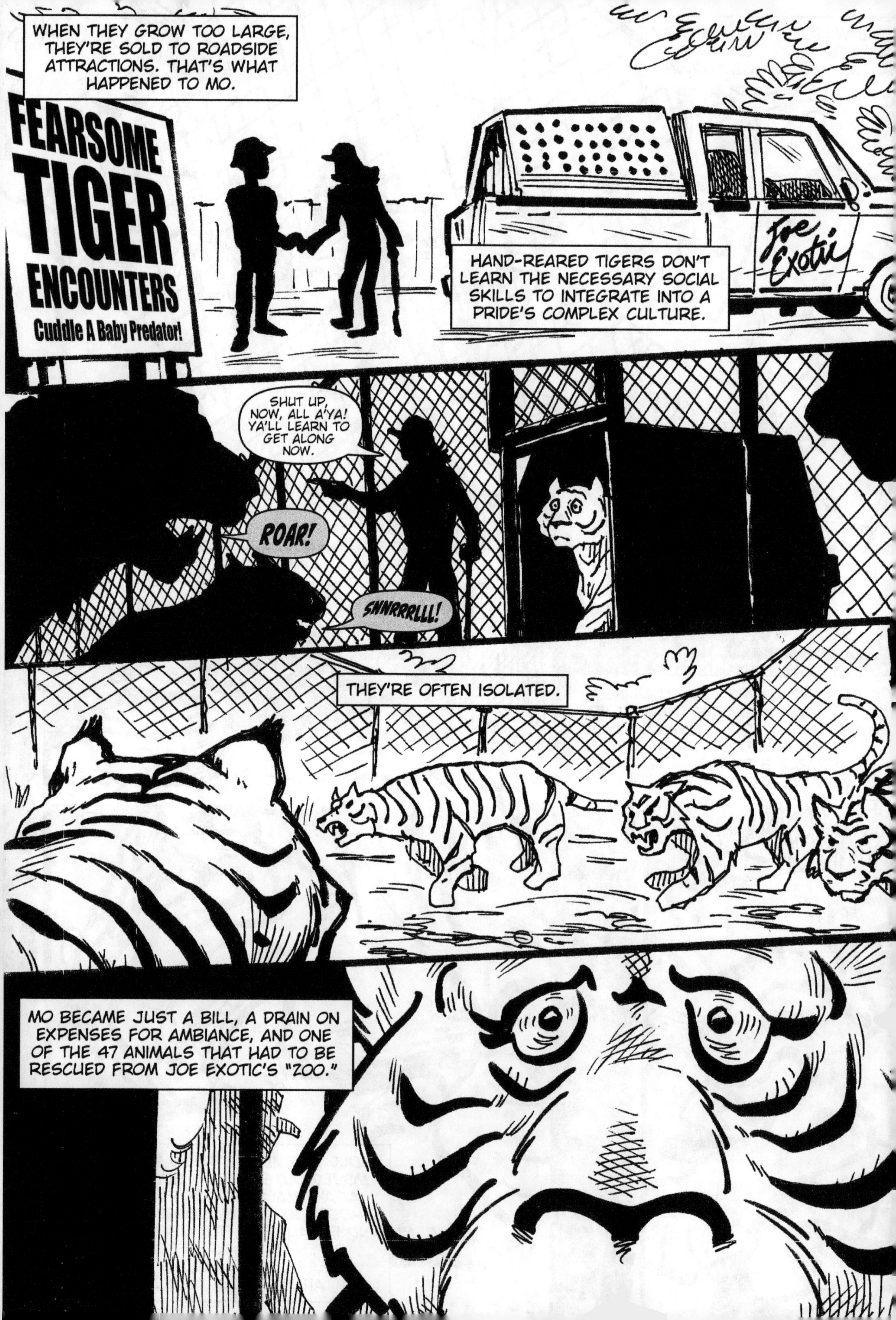
WHEN THEY GROW TOO LARGE, THEY'RE SOLD TO ROADSIDE ATTRACTIONS. THAT'S WHAT HAPPENED TO MO.
FEARSOME TIGER ENCOUNTERS
Cuddle A Baby Predator!
Joe Exotic
HAND-REARED TIGERS DON'T LEARN THE NECESSARY SOCIAL SKILLS TO INTEGRATE INTO A PRIDE'S COMPLEX CULTURE.
SHUT UP, NOW, ALL A'YA! YA'LL LEARN TO GET ALONG NOW.
ROAR!
SNNRRRLLL!
THEY'RE OFTEN ISOLATED.
MO BECAME JUST A BILL, A DRAIN ON EXPENSES FOR AMBIANCE, AND ONE OF THE 47 ANIMALS THAT HAD TO BE RESCUED FROM JOE EXOTIC'S "ZOO."

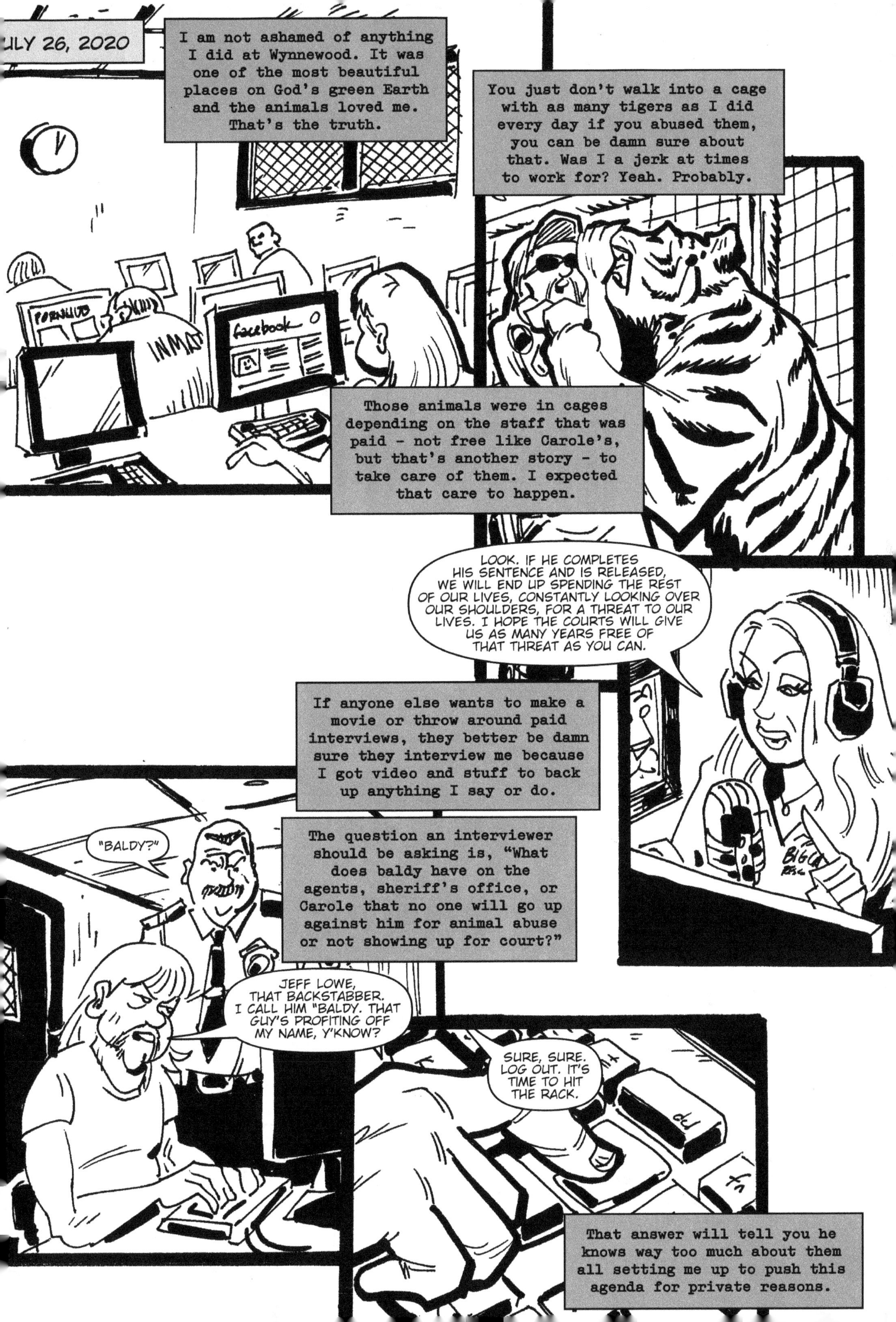

ULY 26, 2020
I am not ashamed of anything I did at Wynnewood. It was one of the most beautiful places on God's green Earth and the animals loved me. That's the truth.
facebook
INMA
You just don't walk into a cage with as many tigers as I did every day if you abused them, you can be damn sure about that. Was I a jerk at times to work for? Yeah. Probably.
Those animals were in cages depending on the staff that was paid - not free like Carole's, but that's another story - to take care of them. I expected that care to happen.
LOOK. IF HE COMPLETES HIS SENTENCE AND IS RELEASED, WE WILL END UP SPENDING THE REST OF OUR LIVES, CONSTANTLY LOOKING OVER OUR SHOULDERS, FOR A THREAT TO OUR LIVES. I HOPE THE COURTS WILL GIVE US AS MANY YEARS FREE OF THAT THREAT AS YOU CAN.
If anyone else wants to make a movie or throw around paid interviews, they better be damn sure they interview me because I got video and stuff to back up anything I say or do.
"BALDY?"
The question an interviewer should be asking is, "What does baldy have on the agents, sheriff's office, or Carole that no one will go up against him for animal abuse or not showing up for court?"
JEFF LOWE, THAT BACKSTABBER. I CALL HIM "BALDY. THAT GUY'S PROFITING OFF MY NAME, Y'KNOW?
SURE, SURE. LOG OUT. IT'S TIME TO HIT THE RACK.
That answer will tell you he knows way too much about them all setting me up to push this agenda for private reasons.

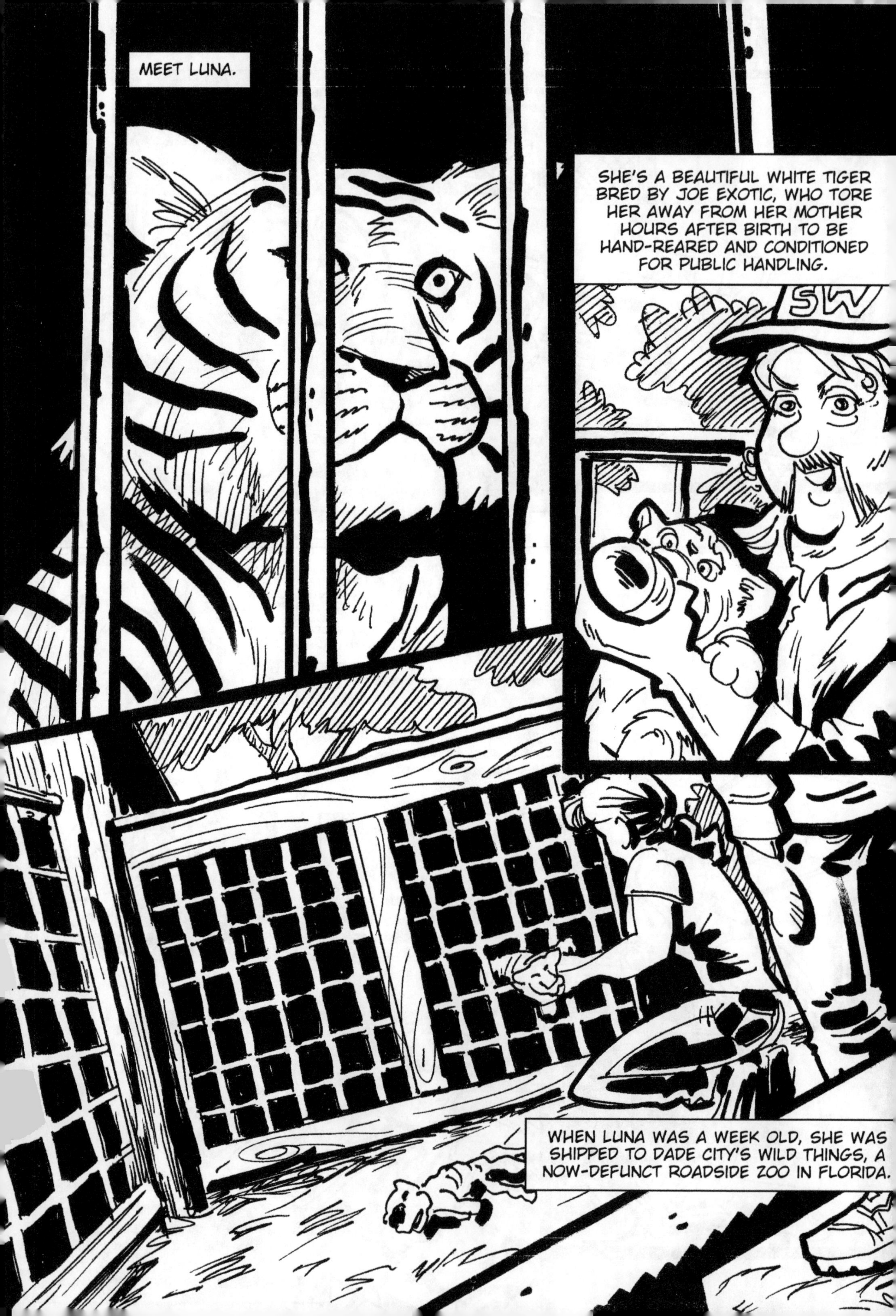
MEET LUNA.
SHE'S A BEAUTIFUL WHITE TIGER BRED BY JOE EXOTIC, WHO TORE HER AWAY FROM HER MOTHER HOURS AFTER BIRTH TO BE HAND-REARED AND CONDITIONED FOR PUBLIC HANDLING.
SW
WHEN LUNA WAS A WEEK OLD, SHE WAS SHIPPED TO DADE CITY'S WILD THINGS, A NOW-DEFUNCT ROADSIDE ZOO IN FLORIDA.

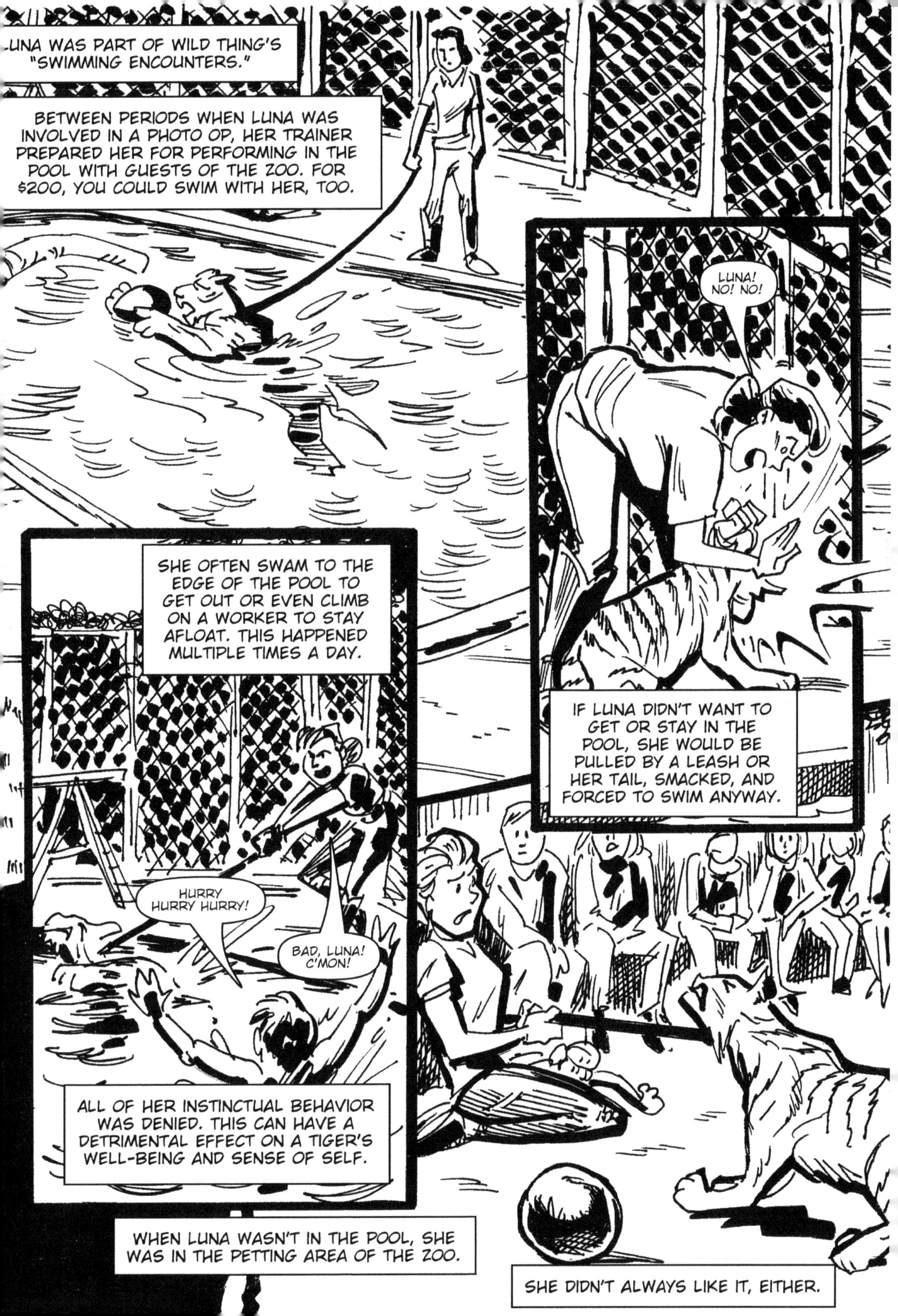
LUNA WAS PART OF WILD THING'S "SWIMMING ENCOUNTERS."
BETWEEN PERIODS WHEN LUNA WAS INVOLVED IN A PHOTO OP, HER TRAINER PREPARED HER FOR PERFORMING IN THE POOL WITH GUESTS OF THE ZOO. FOR $200, YOU COULD SWIM WITH HER, TOO.
LUNA! NO! NO!
IF LUNA DIDN'T WANT TO GET OR STAY IN THE POOL, SHE WOULD BE PULLED BY A LEASH OR HER TAIL, SMACKED, AND FORCED TO SWIM ANYWAY.
SHE OFTEN SWAM TO THE EDGE OF THE POOL TO GET OUT OR EVEN CLIMB ON A WORKER TO STAY AFLOAT. THIS HAPPENED MULTIPLE TIMES A DAY.
HURRY HURRY HURRY!
BAD, LUNA! C'MON!
ALL OF HER INSTINCTUAL BEHAVIOR WAS DENIED. THIS CAN HAVE A DETRIMENTAL EFFECT ON A TIGER'S WELL-BEING AND SENSE OF SELF.
WHEN LUNA WASN'T IN THE POOL, SHE WAS IN THE PETTING AREA OF THE ZOO.
SHE DIDN'T ALWAYS LIKE IT, EITHER.

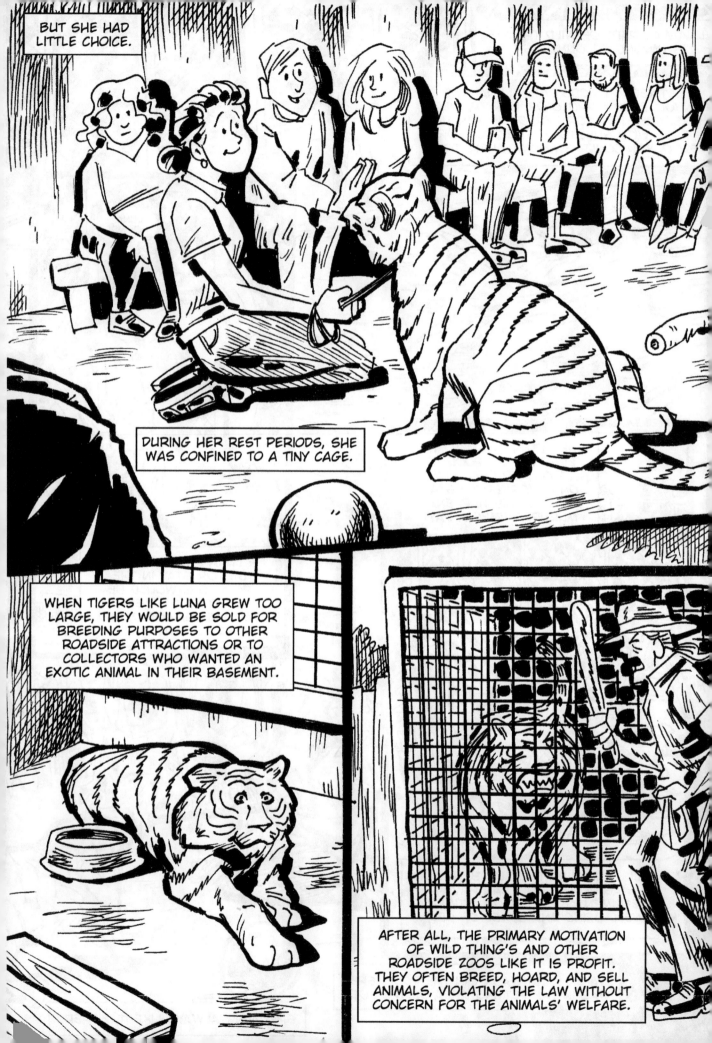

BUT SHE HAD LITTLE CHOICE.

DURING HER REST PERIODS, SHE WAS CONFINED TO A TINY CAGE.

WHEN TIGERS LIKE LUNA GREW TOO LARGE, THEY WOULD BE SOLD FOR BREEDING PURPOSES TO OTHER ROADSIDE ATTRACTIONS OR TO COLLECTORS WHO WANTED AN EXOTIC ANIMAL IN THEIR BASEMENT.

AFTER ALL, THE PRIMARY MOTIVATION OF WILD THING'S AND OTHER ROADSIDE ZOOS LIKE IT IS PROFIT. THEY OFTEN BREED, HOARD, AND SELL ANIMALS, VIOLATING THE LAW WITHOUT CONCERN FOR THE ANIMALS' WELFARE.

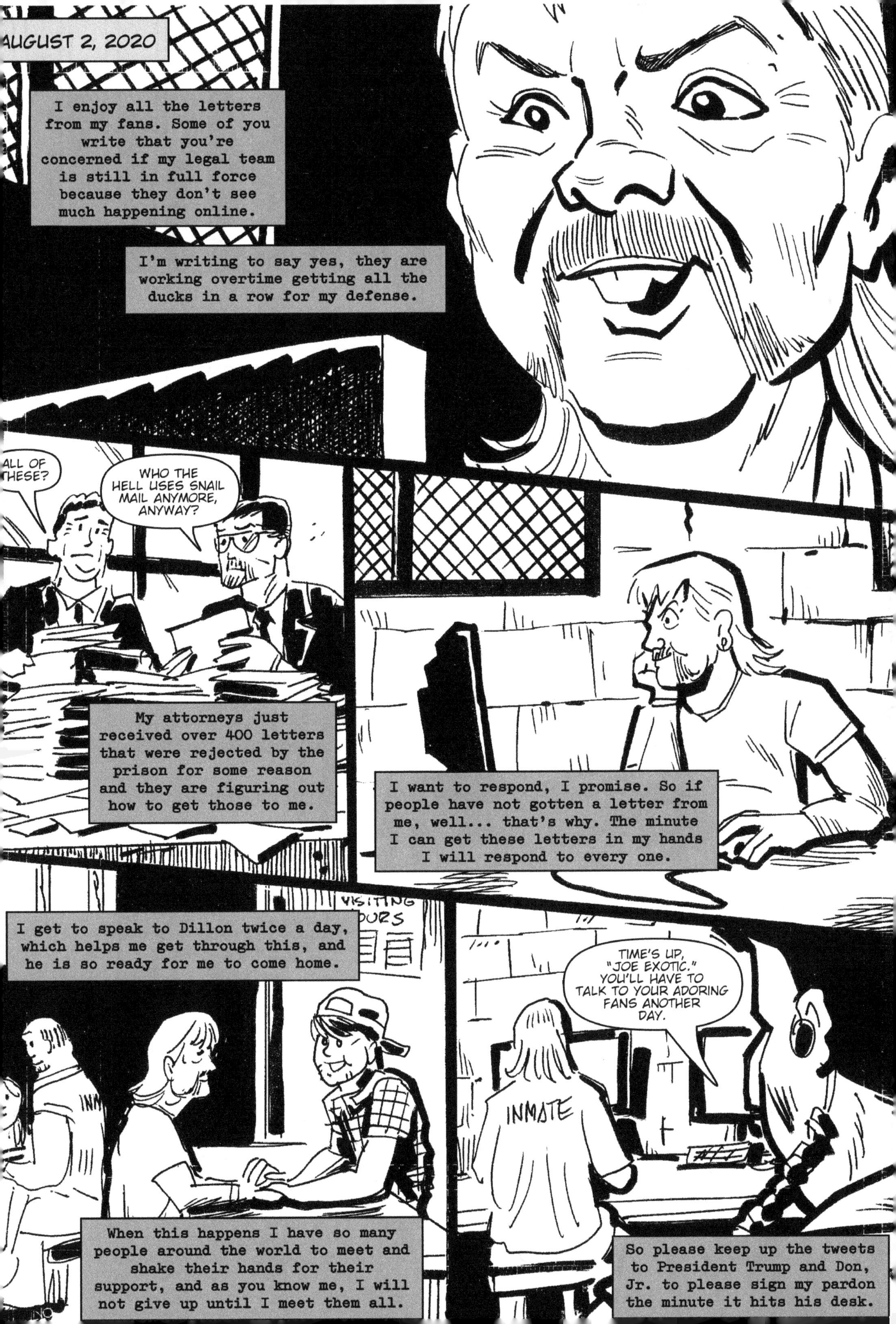

AUGUST 2, 2020
I enjoy all the letters from my fans. Some of you write that you're concerned if my legal team is still in full force because they don't see much happening online.
I'm writing to say yes, they are working overtime getting all the ducks in a row for my defense.
ALL OF THESE?
WHO THE HELL USES SNAIL MAIL ANYMORE, ANYWAY?
My attorneys just received over 400 letters that were rejected by the prison for some reason and they are figuring out how to get those to me.
I want to respond, I promise. So if people have not gotten a letter from me, well... that's why. The minute I can get these letters in my hands I will respond to every one.
I get to speak to Dillon twice a day, which helps me get through this, and he is so ready for me to come home.
VISITING
INMATE
TIME'S UP, "JOE EXOTIC." YOU'LL HAVE TO TALK TO YOUR ADORING FANS ANOTHER DAY.
When this happens I have so many people around the world to meet and shake their hands for their support, and as you know me, I will not give up until I meet them all.
So please keep up the tweets to President Trump and Don, Jr. to please sign my pardon the minute it hits his desk.

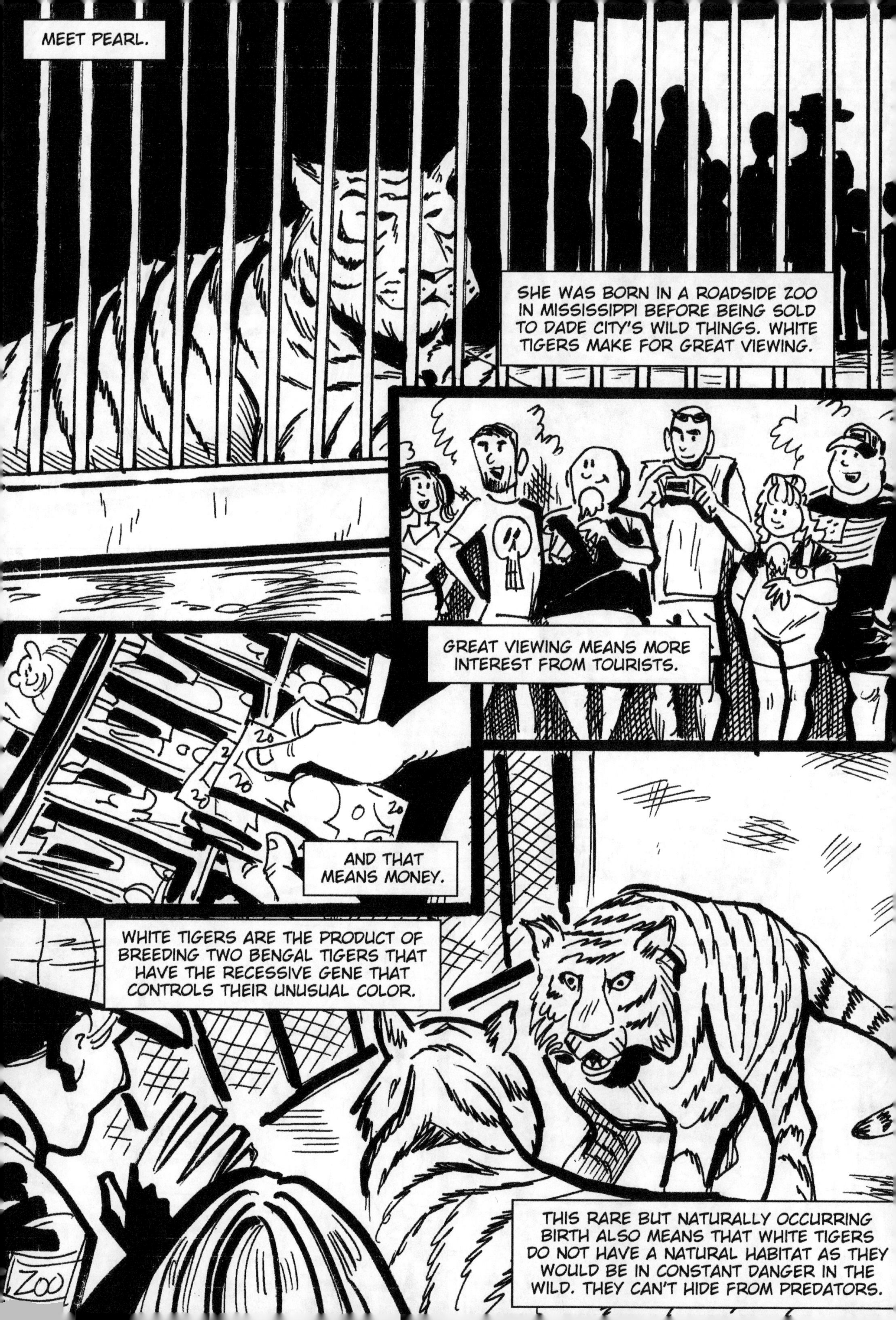
MEET PEARL.
SHE WAS BORN IN A ROADSIDE ZOO IN MISSISSIPPI BEFORE BEING SOLD TO DADE CITY'S WILD THINGS. WHITE TIGERS MAKE FOR GREAT VIEWING.
GREAT VIEWING MEANS MORE INTEREST FROM TOURISTS.
AND THAT MEANS MONEY.
WHITE TIGERS ARE THE PRODUCT OF BREEDING TWO BENGAL TIGERS THAT HAVE THE RECESSIVE GENE THAT CONTROLS THEIR UNUSUAL COLOR.
THIS RARE BUT NATURALLY OCCURRING BIRTH ALSO MEANS THAT WHITE TIGERS DO NOT HAVE A NATURAL HABITAT AS THEY WOULD BE IN CONSTANT DANGER IN THE WILD. THEY CAN'T HIDE FROM PREDATORS.
ZOO

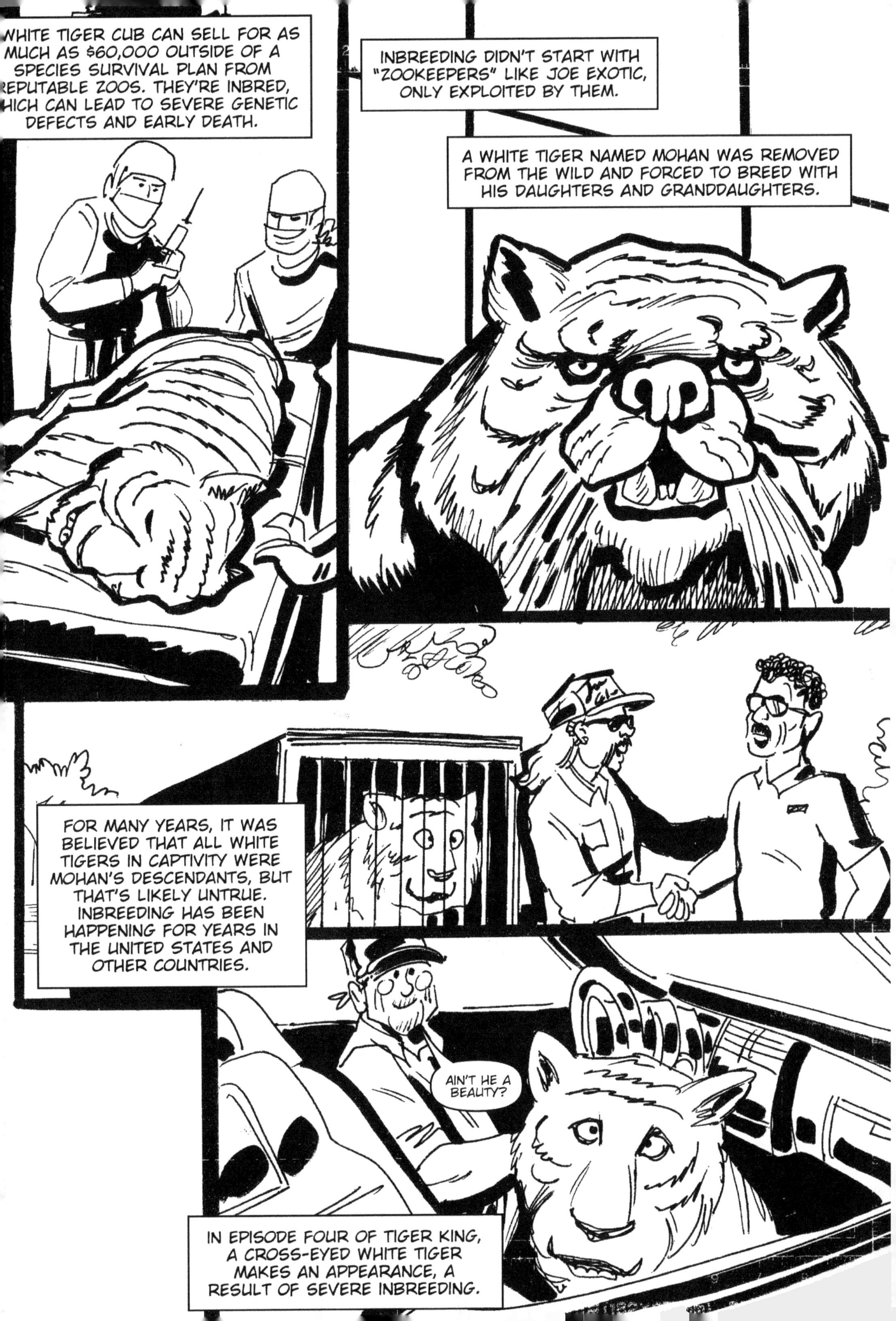
WHITE TIGER CUB CAN SELL FOR AS MUCH AS $60,000 OUTSIDE OF A SPECIES SURVIVAL PLAN FROM REPUTABLE ZOOS. THEY'RE INBRED, WHICH CAN LEAD TO SEVERE GENETIC DEFECTS AND EARLY DEATH.
INBREEDING DIDN'T START WITH "ZOOKEEPERS" LIKE JOE EXOTIC, ONLY EXPLOITED BY THEM.
A WHITE TIGER NAMED MOHAN WAS REMOVED FROM THE WILD AND FORCED TO BREED WITH HIS DAUGHTERS AND GRANDDAUGHTERS.
FOR MANY YEARS, IT WAS BELIEVED THAT ALL WHITE TIGERS IN CAPTIVITY WERE MOHAN'S DESCENDANTS, BUT THAT'S LIKELY UNTRUE. INBREEDING HAS BEEN HAPPENING FOR YEARS IN THE UNITED STATES AND OTHER COUNTRIES.
AIN'T HE A BEAUTY?
IN EPISODE FOUR OF TIGER KING, A CROSS-EYED WHITE TIGER MAKES AN APPEARANCE, A RESULT OF SEVERE INBREEDING.

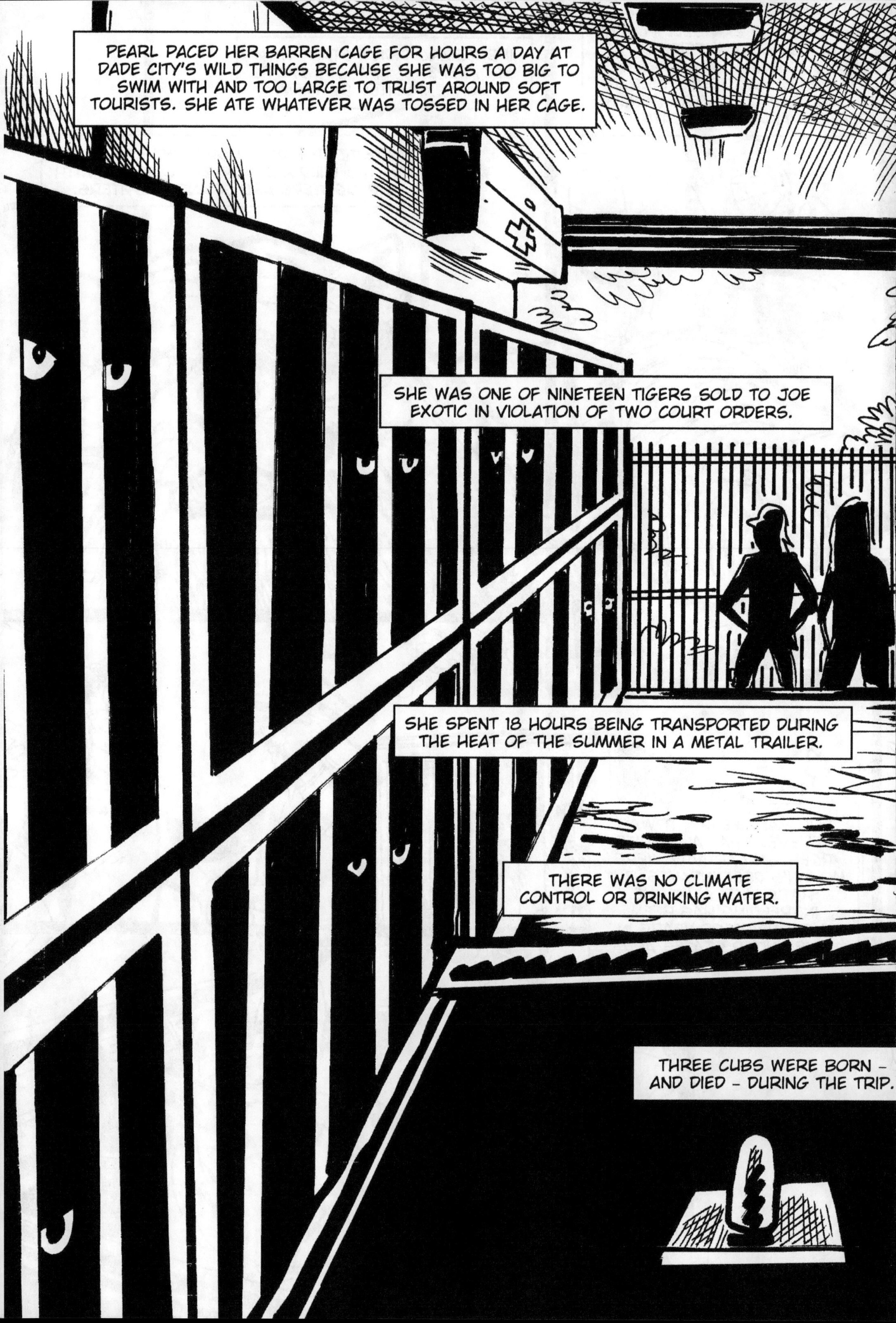
PEARL PACED HER BARREN CAGE FOR HOURS A DAY AT DADE CITY'S WILD THINGS BECAUSE SHE WAS TOO BIG TO SWIM WITH AND TOO LARGE TO TRUST AROUND SOFT TOURISTS. SHE ATE WHATEVER WAS TOSSED IN HER CAGE.
SHE WAS ONE OF NINETEEN TIGERS SOLD TO JOE EXOTIC IN VIOLATION OF TWO COURT ORDERS.
SHE SPENT 18 HOURS BEING TRANSPORTED DURING THE HEAT OF THE SUMMER IN A METAL TRAILER.
THERE WAS NO CLIMATE CONTROL OR DRINKING WATER.
THREE CUBS WERE BORN – AND DIED – DURING THE TRIP.

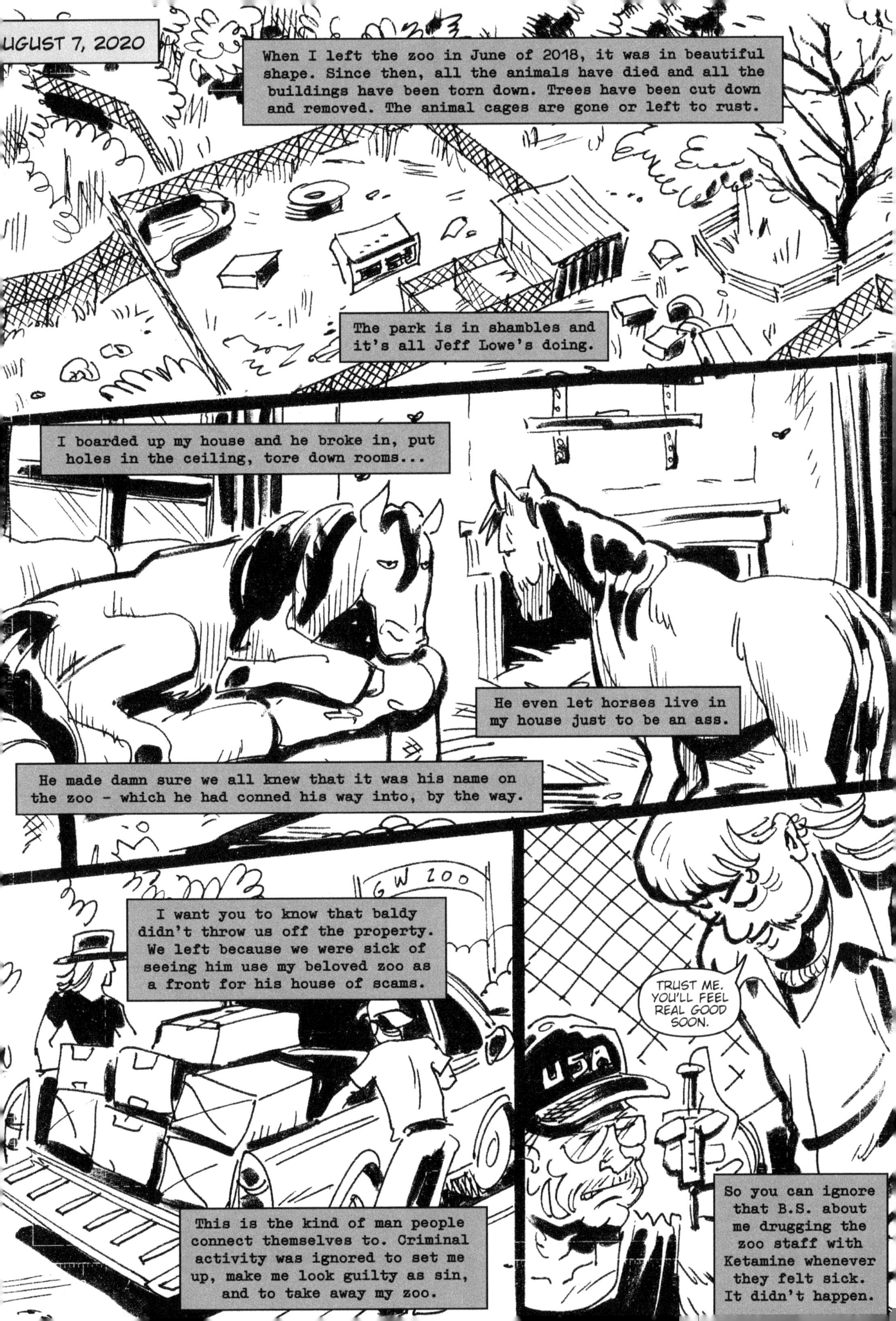
UGUST 7, 2020
When I left the zoo in June of 2018, it was in beautiful shape. Since then, all the animals have died and all the buildings have been torn down. Trees have been cut down and removed. The animal cages are gone or left to rust.
The park is in shambles and it's all Jeff Lowe's doing.
I boarded up my house and he broke in, put holes in the ceiling, tore down rooms...
He even let horses live in my house just to be an ass.
He made damn sure we all knew that it was his name on the zoo - which he had conned his way into, by the way.
GW ZOO
I want you to know that baldy didn't throw us off the property. We left because we were sick of seeing him use my beloved zoo as a front for his house of scams.
This is the kind of man people connect themselves to. Criminal activity was ignored to set me up, make me look guilty as sin, and to take away my zoo.
TRUST ME. YOU'LL FEEL REAL GOOD SOON.
USA
So you can ignore that B.S. about me drugging the zoo staff with Ketamine whenever they felt sick. It didn't happen.

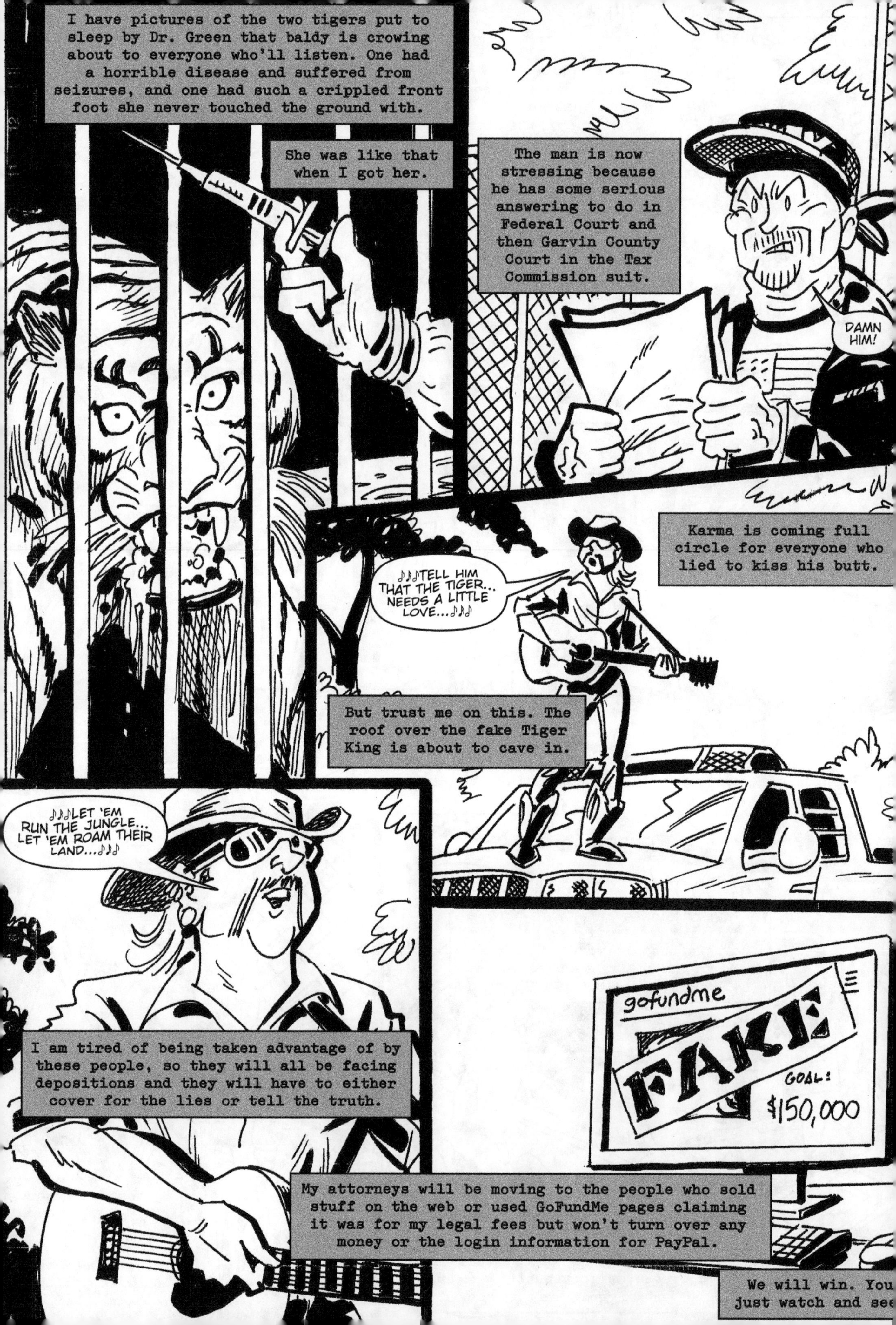

I have pictures of the two tigers put to sleep by Dr. Green that baldy is crowing about to everyone who'll listen. One had a horrible disease and suffered from seizures, and one had such a crippled front foot she never touched the ground with.
She was like that when I got her.
The man is now stressing because he has some serious answering to do in Federal Court and then Garvin County Court in the Tax Commission suit.
DAMN HIM!
♪♪♪TELL HIM THAT THE TIGER... NEEDS A LITTLE LOVE...♪♪♪
Karma is coming full circle for everyone who lied to kiss his butt.
But trust me on this. The roof over the fake Tiger King is about to cave in.
♪♪♪LET 'EM RUN THE JUNGLE... LET 'EM ROAM THEIR LAND...♪♪♪
I am tired of being taken advantage of by these people, so they will all be facing depositions and they will have to either cover for the lies or tell the truth.
gofundme
FAKE
GOAL:
$150,000
My attorneys will be moving to the people who sold stuff on the web or used GoFundMe pages claiming it was for my legal fees but won't turn over any money or the login information for PayPal.
We will win. You just watch and se

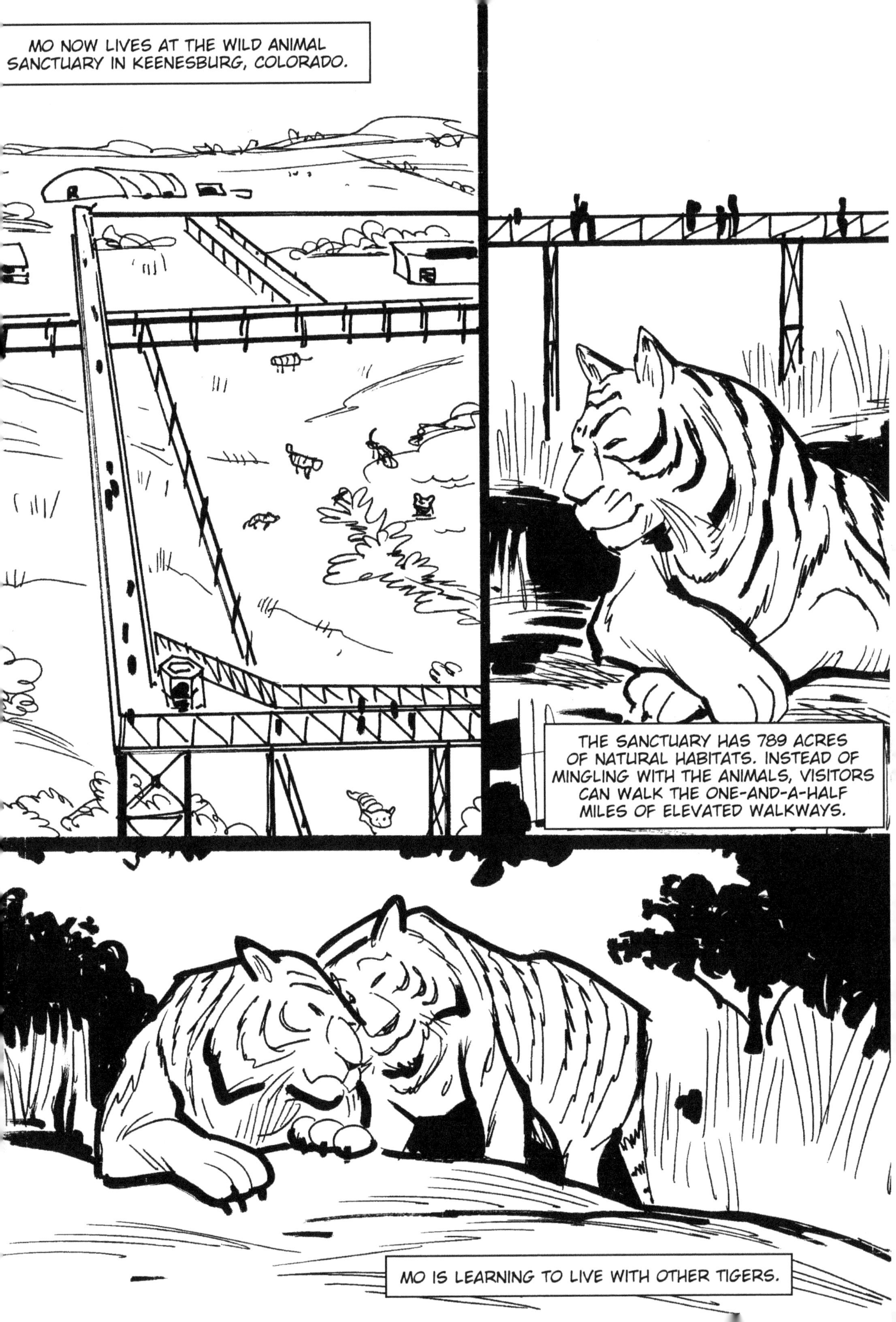
MO NOW LIVES AT THE WILD ANIMAL SANCTUARY IN KEENESBURG, COLORADO.
THE SANCTUARY HAS 789 ACRES OF NATURAL HABITATS. INSTEAD OF MINGLING WITH THE ANIMALS, VISITORS CAN WALK THE ONE-AND-A-HALF MILES OF ELEVATED WALKWAYS.
MO IS LEARNING TO LIVE WITH OTHER TIGERS.

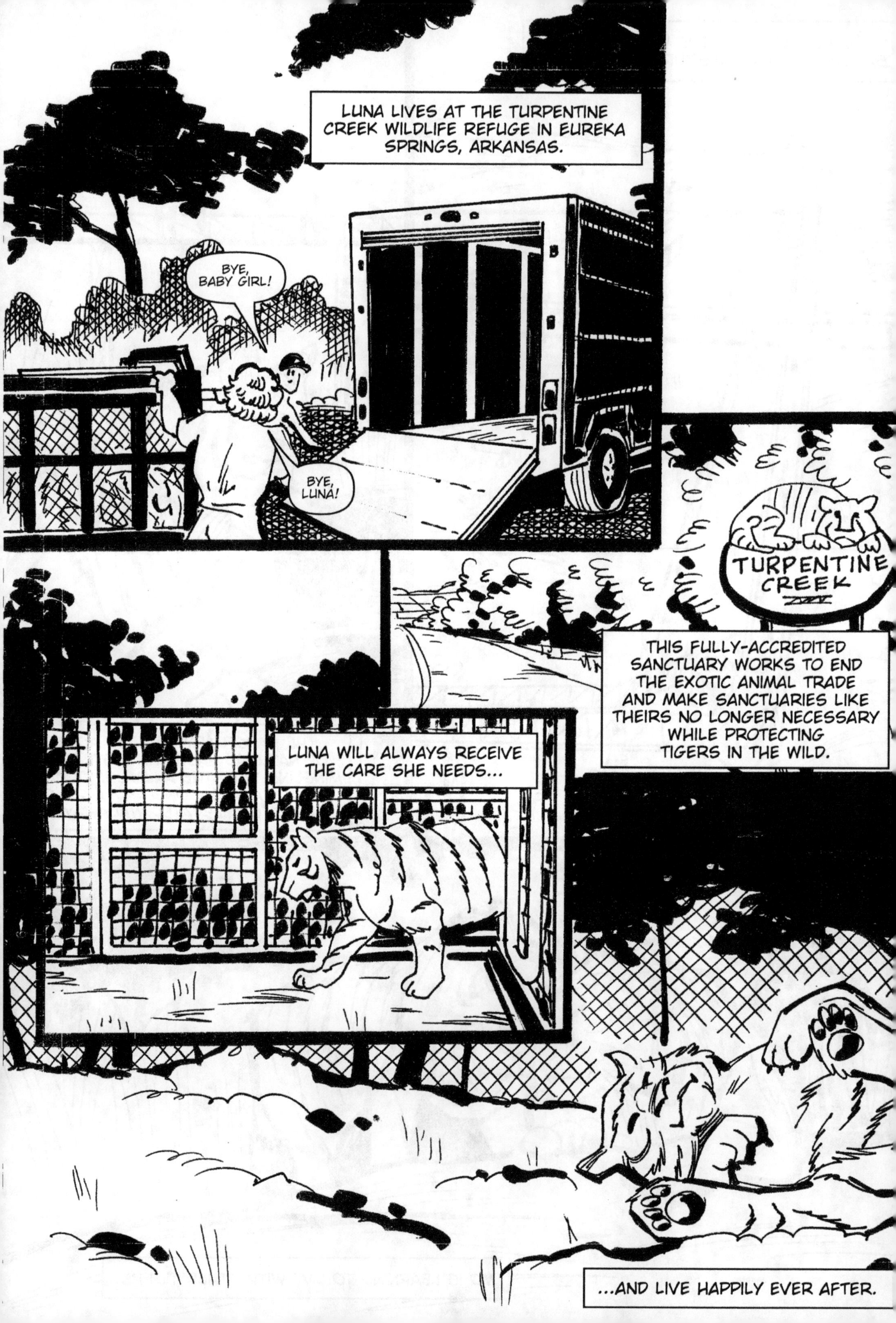
LUNA LIVES AT THE TURPENTINE CREEK WILDLIFE REFUGE IN EUREKA SPRINGS, ARKANSAS.
BYE, BABY GIRL!
BYE, LUNA!
TURPENTINE CREEK
THIS FULLY-ACCREDITED SANCTUARY WORKS TO END THE EXOTIC ANIMAL TRADE AND MAKE SANCTUARIES LIKE THEIRS NO LONGER NECESSARY WHILE PROTECTING TIGERS IN THE WILD.
LUNA WILL ALWAYS RECEIVE THE CARE SHE NEEDS...
...AND LIVE HAPPILY EVER AFTER.

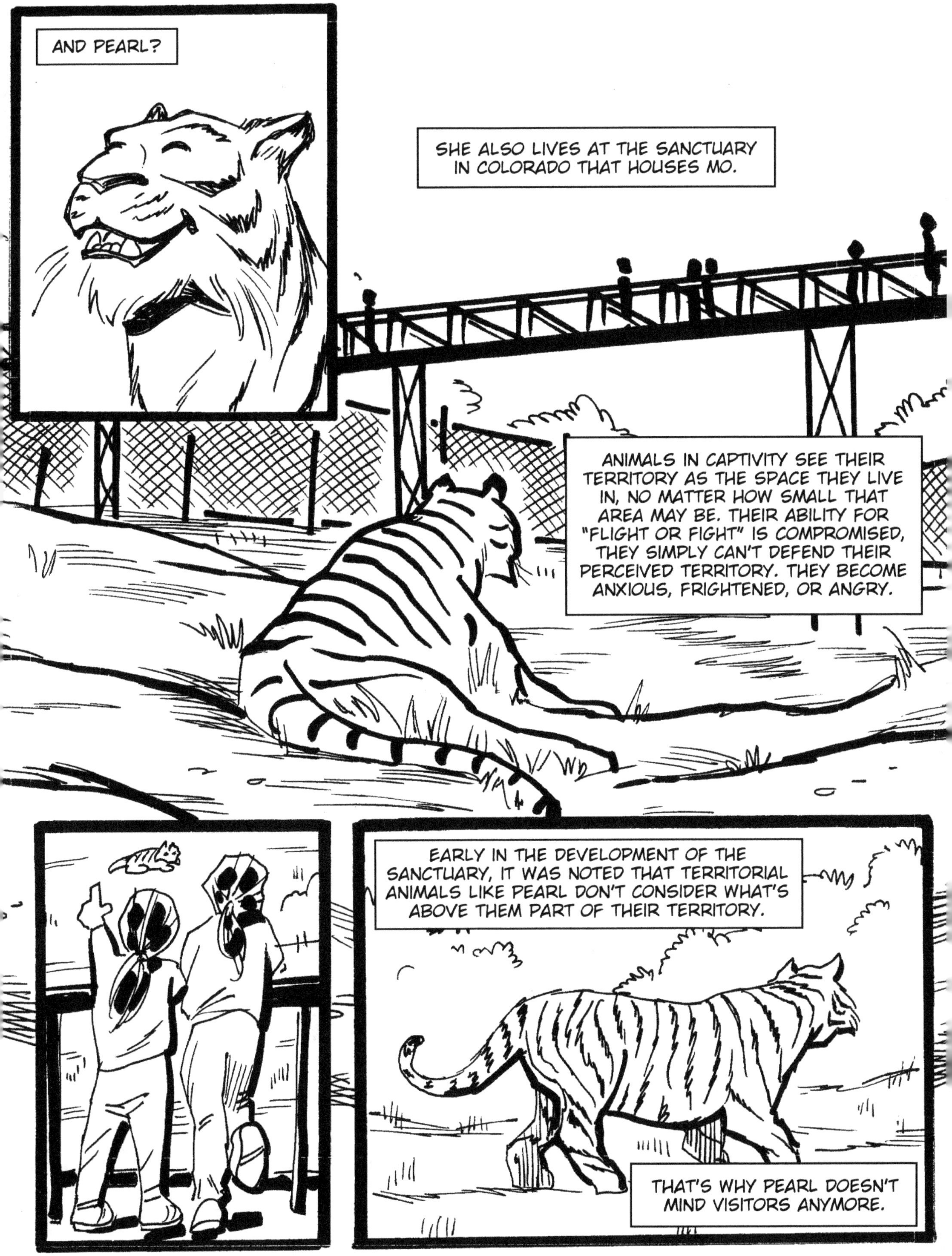
AND PEARL?
SHE ALSO LIVES AT THE SANCTUARY IN COLORADO THAT HOUSES MO.
ANIMALS IN CAPTIVITY SEE THEIR TERRITORY AS THE SPACE THEY LIVE IN, NO MATTER HOW SMALL THAT AREA MAY BE. THEIR ABILITY FOR "FLIGHT OR FIGHT" IS COMPROMISED, THEY SIMPLY CAN'T DEFEND THEIR PERCEIVED TERRITORY. THEY BECOME ANXIOUS, FRIGHTENED, OR ANGRY.
EARLY IN THE DEVELOPMENT OF THE SANCTUARY, IT WAS NOTED THAT TERRITORIAL ANIMALS LIKE PEARL DON'T CONSIDER WHAT'S ABOVE THEM PART OF THEIR TERRITORY.
THAT'S WHY PEARL DOESN'T MIND VISITORS ANYMORE.

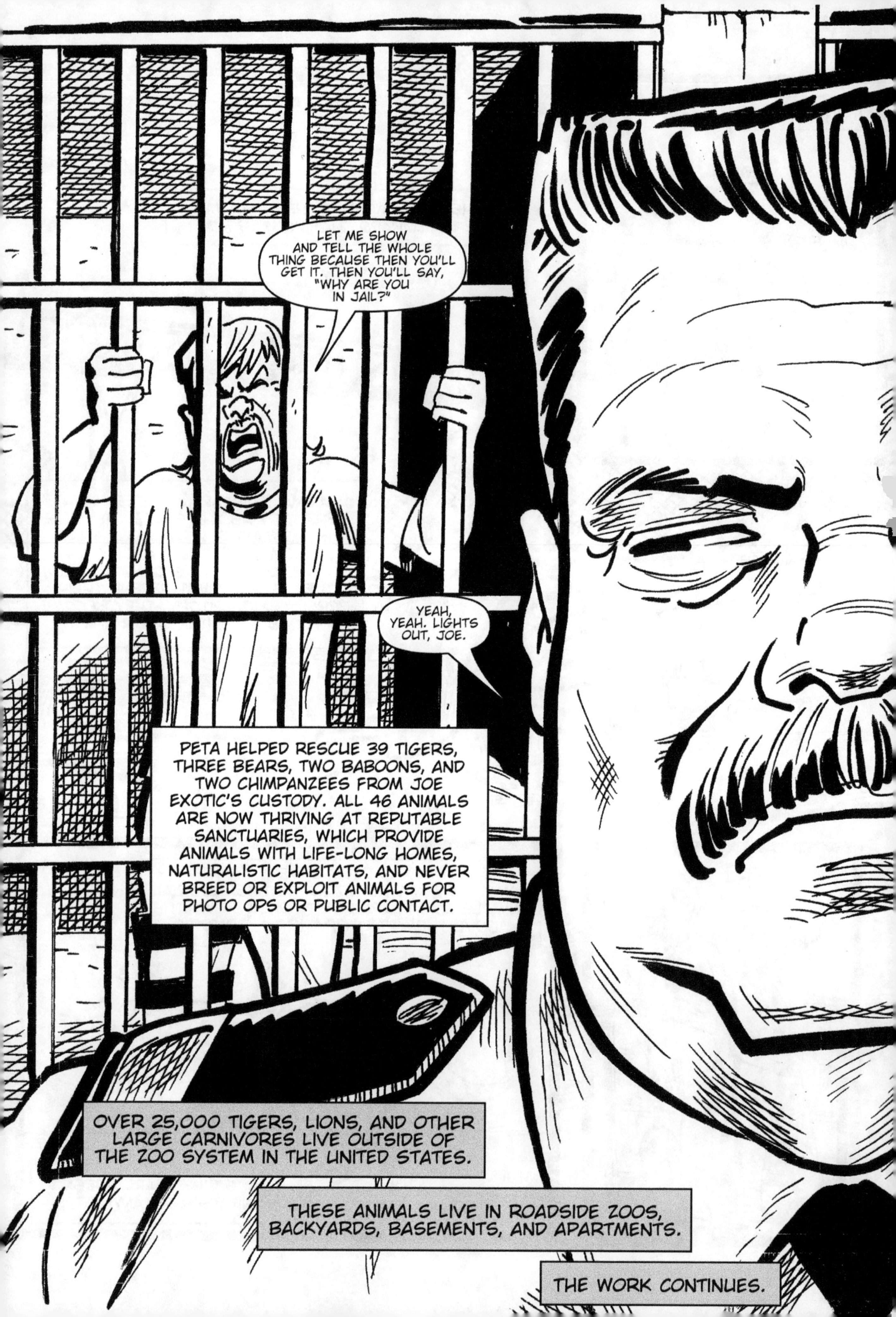
LET ME SHOW AND TELL THE WHOLE THING BECAUSE THEN YOU'LL GET IT. THEN YOU'LL SAY, "WHY ARE YOU IN JAIL?"
YEAH, YEAH. LIGHTS OUT, JOE.
PETA HELPED RESCUE 39 TIGERS, THREE BEARS, TWO BABOONS, AND TWO CHIMPANZEES FROM JOE EXOTIC'S CUSTODY. ALL 46 ANIMALS ARE NOW THRIVING AT REPUTABLE SANCTUARIES, WHICH PROVIDE ANIMALS WITH LIFE-LONG HOMES, NATURALISTIC HABITATS, AND NEVER BREED OR EXPLOIT ANIMALS FOR PHOTO OPS OR PUBLIC CONTACT.
OVER 25,000 TIGERS, LIONS, AND OTHER LARGE CARNIVORES LIVE OUTSIDE OF THE ZOO SYSTEM IN THE UNITED STATES.
THESE ANIMALS LIVE IN ROADSIDE ZOOS, BACKYARDS, BASEMENTS, AND APARTMENTS.
THE WORK CONTINUES.

Can you help
Joe Exotic get
meat for his **tigers?**

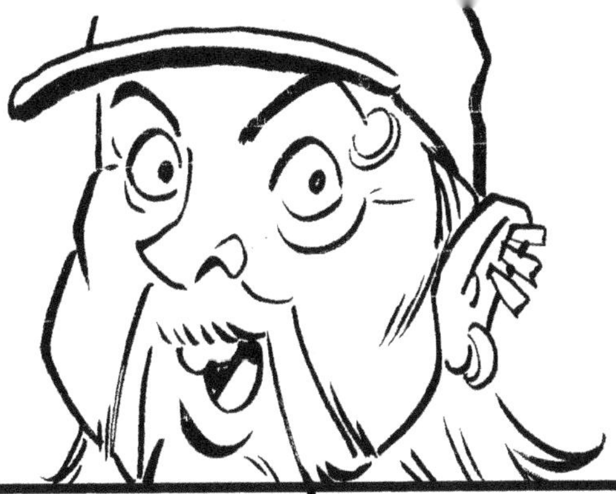

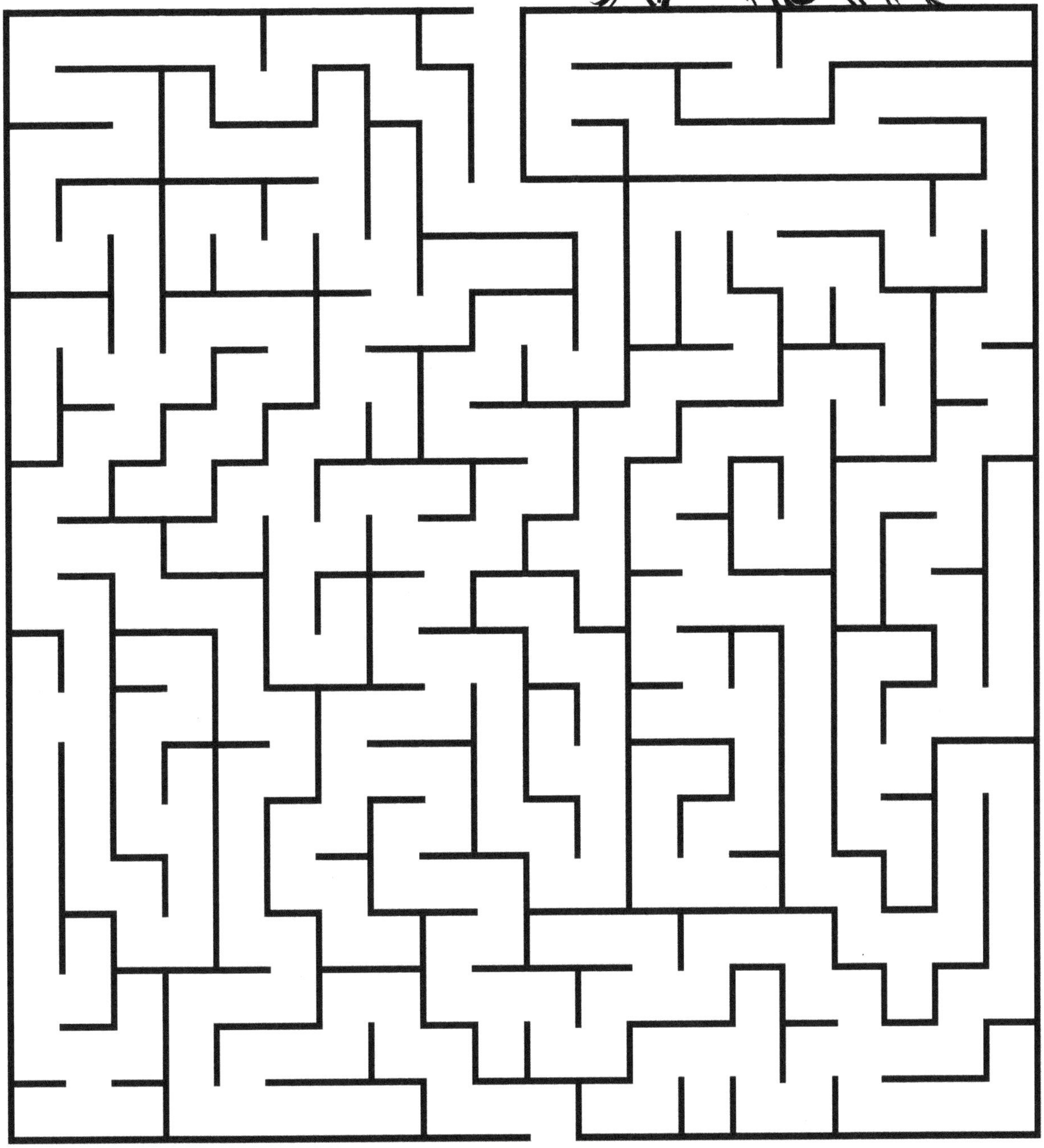

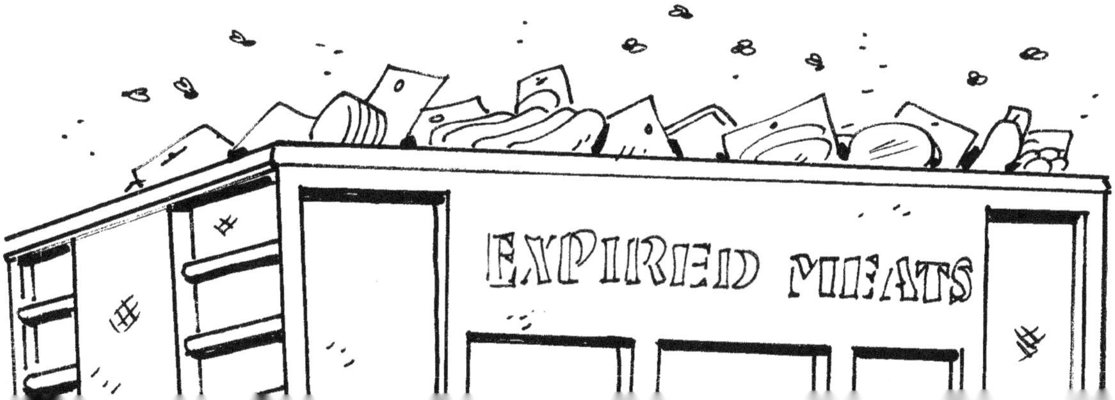
EXPIRED MEATS

Can you find the ingredients to make **CRYSTAL METH?**

```
L S C C O F Q I S P L C G V P
R I U A M M O N I A D I O S T
B X T R Z R B B E G X R E V O
I W C H O L D T X W H U A A L
A U C A I H G C H I D F S S U
W U C C N U P X O O E L G K E
B I C N I Q M S E N O U V K N
D N A L Y Y U P O D E S O A E
F R B V J A H T A H K P S C V
M O K W U E E V E V P D H R F
A X D Z D C E Y L E E N R Y M
U H E R A Z A Q D I N Z X Z C
V R I R W B V E Z D P C W U P
D N C I R O L H C O R D Y H R
E W H Q S H Q E P L F P D U M
```

ACETONE   LYE

ACID   PHOSPHORUS

AMMONIA   PSEUDOEPHEDRINE

HYDROCHLORIC   SULFURIC

LITHIUM   TOLUENE

TIDALWAVE COMICS

Michael Frizell — Writer

Joe Paradise — Pencils

Ben Glibert — Letters

Darren G. Davis — Editor

Joe Paradise — Cover

Darren G. Davis
Publisher

Maggie Jessup
Publicity

Susan Ferris
Entertainment Manager

TIDALWAVE PRODUCTIONS

PRINTED IN THE USA www.tidalwavecomics.com

CPSIA information can be obtained
at www.ICGtesting.com
Printed in the USA
BVHW050259121121
621447BV00021B/397

9 781954 044999